THE AMAZING GRACE DEVOTIONAL

THE AMAZING GRACE DEVOTIONAL

Shoes, Belly Fat, Linen Underwear, And Other Interesting Stuff

52 devotional readings to strengthen your faith walk

Tom Kempf

Copyright © 2016 **Tom Kempf**
All rights reserved.

ISBN-13: **9781539032700**
ISBN-10: **1539032701**

Table of Contents

About the Author · vii
Preface· xi

These Shoes Were Made For Walkin' · · · · · · · · · · · · · · · · · ·1
Runaway Bride· ·5
He Makes All Things New ·9
Are You "Second?" ·13
Batteries Not Included ·15
"Bye-bye, Stubborn Belly Fat!" ·18
Burned! ·22
Chalkboard Salvation ·25
Welcome To the Complaint Department: · · · · · · · · · · · · · · ·29
From One Clay Pot to Another ·32
How To Handle Difficult People ·34
Simply Forgiven· ·38
Are You Disillusioned? Good! ·42
The Battle Regarding Divine Healing · · · · · · · · · · · · · · · · ·45
Why Doesn't God DO Something? · · · · · · · · · · · · · · · · · 48
Let's Get Those Ducks In A Row · · · · · · · · · · · · · · · · · · ·51
You Are The Same As Jesus ·55
I Can Forgive, But I'll Never Forget· · · · · · · · · · · · · · · · · ·58
The Freedom Of God's Grace· ·61
Fruit Juice Saints—Just Squeeze · · · · · · · · · · · · · · · · · 64
Do You Know Right From Wrong? · · · · · · · · · · · · · · · · · · ·67

Guilty As Charged · 71
Are You Hungry and Thirsty? · · · · · · · · · · · · · · · · · ·75
The Hyper-Grace Loophole ·78
I Love The Church—But Which One? · · · · · · · · · · ·81
Everything Is Possible With God · · · · · · · · · · · · · · · 84
Law Living Is Not Fun Living · · · · · · · · · · · · · · · · · 88
When God Got His Hands Dirty · · · · · · · · · · · · · · ·91
Let There Be Light! ·94
Who Wears Linen Underwear? · · · · · · · · · · · · · · · · ·98
The Love Of Grace ·101
Lunchtime Seeds—A Short Drama · · · · · · · · · · · ·104
Must I Forgive To Be Forgiven? · · · · · · · · · · · · · · ·109
Who's Guarding Your Gates? · · · · · · · · · · · · · · · · · 112
No Fear · 116
"Obedience" Is A Four-Letter Word · · · · · · · · · · · 119
On Being Offended · 122
Simplicity In Prayer · 125
The Real Love Boat · 129
The Rating Game · 133
A Herd Of Sacred Cows · 136
The Caravan Is On Its Way! · · · · · · · · · · · · · · · · · · 139
The Trap Of Self-Righteousness · · · · · · · · · · · · · · 143
Are You Living In The Shadows? · · · · · · · · · · · · · 147
How To Discover The Will Of God · · · · · · · · · · · 150
Power To Fly · 154
To Tithe Or Not to Tithe · 157
Love Those Mountaintop Experiences! · · · · · · · · 161
What Are You Full Of? · 164
What? Me Worry? · 167
The WWJD Acting School · · · · · · · · · · · · · · · · · · 170
Put Jesus Back In The Classroom? · · · · · · · · · · · · 172

Author Biography · 177

About the Author

Tom Kempf lives in Florida with his wife, Nancy, and a little black dog named Mei-Ling. He grew up in Minnesota, has lived in Illinois and Massachusetts, and has been a businessman, magazine editor, church pastor for twenty-three years, and Bible teacher. He enjoys writing, Bible teaching, preaching and flying radio-controlled model aircraft.

He was ordained and was the founding pastor of a denominational church in 1987. Tom resigned from the church in 2010 to pursue a simpler church expression in less formal settings such as homes and small groups.

Dedication

To my wife, Nancy, who truly lights up my life. I love her so much that if she ever leaves me, I'm going with her.

Preface

It's short, so take a moment to read it and get inside my head.

I'm in full agreement with Paul, the apostle, when he wrote, *"My life is worth nothing to me unless I use it for finishing the work assigned me by the Lord Jesus—the work of telling others the Good News about the wonderful grace of God." (Acts 20:24 NLT)*

I want this devotional book to encourage you to thoroughly embrace the freedom available in God's grace through Jesus Christ. And if you're not sure about where you stand with Him, I hope it will encourage you to open your mind and heart to the truth of the Gospel.

This collection is based on some of the teachings I've presented in the past few years, condensed for quick and easy reading. There's bound to be some repetition because I come at single topics from several different directions. I've had fun with a few of the articles, and I believe you'll find them easy to read and understand. I pray they will help you to live your Christian life with confidence and joy.

I have tapped many sources for these articles. The Bible, the Holy Spirit, prayer, and fellowship with other believers have all provided me with valuable insight. God has also blessed the church with teachers, people who have the ability to understand spiritual truth and communicate it accurately. I have received helpful understanding from several gifted Bible teachers. I can't always remember from whom I got some of my examples, but I do credit those I can identify. My thanks to all of them!

The Gospel is simple. As Paul said, it's the Gospel—the Good News—about the wonderful grace of God. Jesus Christ, full of grace and truth, was the very personification of grace. In fact, the main topic of the entire New Covenant is the super-abounding grace of God. The New King James Version of the Bible mentions grace more than 120 times in the New Covenant.

I'm concerned that much of the church has put a veil over the simple Gospel, keeping it out of focus for many. *(See 2Corinthians 3:15-16)* Paul, the apostle, said it well, *"I fear, lest somehow, as the serpent deceived Eve by his craftiness, so your minds may be corrupted from the simplicity that is in Christ." (2Corinthians 11:3 NKJV)*

The chapters are too short to dig to great depths of teaching, but perhaps you will be motivated to do as the Bereans did after Paul taught them the Gospel of grace.

And the people of Berea ... listened eagerly to Paul's message. They searched the Scriptures day after day to see if Paul and Silas were teaching the truth. (Acts 17:11 NLT)

Finally, I quote modern Bible translations because they use clear language that makes them easy to understand. I quote from these Bible versions and use the following abbreviations:

New King James Version = NKJV

New Living Translation = NLT

While I appreciate the tremendous blessing the King James Version has been to the Kingdom of God, its archaic language is difficult for many.

Bless you as you seek to know Him more and to experience the freedom He has provided! *So if the Son sets you free, you are truly free. (John 8:36 NLT)*

Tom Kempf

These Shoes Were Made For Walkin'

I was intrigued by the topic of shoes one day after reading about Moses and the burning bush in *Exodus 3*. A quick look through our closet revealed dress shoes, deck shoes, sandals, walking shoes, gym shoes, bowling shoes, golf shoes, loafers (occasionally one of my wife's pet names for me), work boots, and even a pair of really cool cowboy boots.

If I searched your closet, what would I find? Galoshes, corrective shoes, children's shoes, waders, Kermit-the-Frog slippers, tap shoes, baseball shoes? One thing for sure—a number of people have many pairs of shoes, each for a specific purpose or occasion.

Moses wore expensive shoes during his forty years as a prince of Egypt but had to switch to rugged sandals during the next forty years as a lowly shepherd in the land of Midian. One day, while leading his sheep in the desert, he saw a burning bush which wasn't really burning. Oh, there were flames alright, but the bush remained unscorched.

Moses walked over to check it out, and he heard a voice.
God called to him from within the bush, "Moses! Moses!"
And Moses said, "Here I am."
"Do not come any closer," God said. "Take off your sandals, for the place where you are standing is holy ground." (Exodus 3:4-5 NLT)

Moses stood barefoot before God and received his marching orders.

So now, go. I am sending you to Pharaoh to bring my people the Israelites out of Egypt." (Exodus 3:10 NLT)

Let's fast forward 40 years or so. Israel was free from Egypt, Moses had died, and Joshua was ready to lead the nation of Israel across the Jordan River to occupy the Promised Land.

When Joshua went alone to look at Jericho, the first city to be conquered, an angel stood in front of him with a drawn sword. The angel identified himself as the commander of the Lord's army. He commanded Joshua, *"Take off your sandals, for the place where you are standing is holy." (Joshua 5:15 NLT)*

Now Joshua stood barefoot before God and received his marching orders. For six days Israel was to march around Jericho once each day. On the seventh day, they were to march around the city seven times, with the priests blowing the trumpets, and end with a shout! The final day ended in victory for Israel. *(See Joshua 6:1-5)*

Both Moses and Joshua experienced something revolutionary. I believe both were early appearances of Jesus Christ, the grace of God at work in the Old Testament. Neither of these men was perfect in his behavior, but both were willing to step out in faith as God commanded. God chose to accomplish His purposes through them. The point God made to each man was, "Take off your shoes, transfer ownership to Me, and then put them back on. Now they're *My* shoes on *your* feet. It's not *your* skill, power, or direction now, but *Mine." (See Galatians 2:20)*

All our shoes have natural purposes. But when God owns them and we step out at His command, the purposes become *super*natural. Our whole outlook changes as we move ahead under His leadership. When we walk the aisles at the grocery store, our reason for being there changes. We're no longer there simply to buy bread, milk, and hamburger. We're there to represent Jesus Christ, and while we're there we'll pick up some bread, milk, and hamburger.

To keep our own joy, victory, freedom and authority in Christ we need to take our natural shoes off, give them to Him and put them back on. God's grace transforms our natural shoes into power shoes. The armor of God includes shoes, too:

Stand firm… with your feet fitted with the readiness that comes from the gospel of peace." (Ephesians 6:14-15 NKJV)

God wants us to walk through life in Gospel Shoes, with the Holy Spirit as our guide and source of strength. However, we wander from His path when we slip back into our own shoes and take control. Our flesh closets are full of shoes we drag out from time to time. We can "stand firm" in our Gospel Shoes every time we are tempted to abandon them for shoes that don't match our spiritual outfit.

When offended we want to put on our Combat Boots. We resist loving our enemies, don't want to bless those who curse us and avoid doing good to those who hate us. We don't want to put on God's Forgiveness Slippers.

There are the Money Shoes. They pinch with selfishness and fear, but we keep them on because they give us security. Wearing them keeps us from putting on God's Generosity Shoes. Loving our Money Shoes can lead to all kinds of trouble.

And look! There are our Fun Shoes. They take us to the movies, the clubs, the TV room, the music sources, YouTube, and other fun spots. These activities aren't wrong in themselves, but if we're not careful about their content, we'll miss out on the Peace Shoes that God has provided for us.

Don't forget those Sexy Shoes. They're deceptively comfortable, and we slip them on when we want to indulge our sexual desires outside of God's guidelines. They keep us from being content with our spouses or our singleness, and we can fall into all kinds of traps. God has Purity Shoes for us if we'll make sure to put them on.

Then there are Time Shoes, Religious Shoes, Busy Shoes, and many more in the flesh closet.

Moses argued with God at the burning bush. He didn't want to give up ownership of comfortable sandals. When he considered

God's assignment, he protested, "Send someone else!" Sounds familiar to me—how about you? Maybe you've avoided God's call and have been walking in your own shoes all your life. Well, God is speaking right now, saying, "Take off your shoes and give Me ownership of them. Change your mind about Jesus and simply believe. Be born again and come—follow Him." *(See John 3 and Romans 10:9)*

Or maybe you're a believer with a few pairs of shoes you need to turn over to God. Let Him have control of your Combat Boots, Fun Shoes, Sexy Shoes, Time Shoes, Busy Shoes, and the rest.

We need to stop sneaking out of the house into the darkness with the wrong shoes on. God's grace brings about a miraculous transformation and encouragement:

For once you were full of darkness, but now you have light from the Lord. So live as people of light! For this light within you produces only what is good and right and true. (Ephesians 5:8-9 NLT)

God's shoes are all Good News shoes. The Bible, the word of God, is a lamp to our feet and light to our paths. In addition, these shoes fit perfectly because they are custom made for each of His children. Wear them with trust and joy!

Runaway Bride

This is a true story. Back in 2005, John Mason was engaged to be married to Jennifer Wilbanks. There were six hundred wedding guests on their way, and all twelve of the bridesmaids and the twelve groomsmen were prepared to do their part. It was to be a very expensive wedding.

But Jennifer disappeared just before the wedding, sparking a nationwide bride hunt. John Mason was suspected of foul play, and hundreds of volunteers searched nearby locations. A few days later, Jennifer showed up, unharmed except for cold feet.

She simply ran away. She said she was aware of her imperfections and felt that she could not be the wife her fiancé needed. Even after this disaster, John Mason said he would still marry her.

The Bible teaches that the Church, as a body, and every born-again believer, individually, is the bride of Jesus Christ.

He [Jesus] gave up his life for her [the church] to make her holy and clean, washed by baptism and God's word. He did this to present her to himself as a glorious church without a spot or wrinkle or any other blemish. Instead, she will be holy and without fault. (Ephesians 5:25-27 NLT)

The first problem with Jennifer Wilbanks was fear of her imperfections.

Sometimes we believers run from Jesus, leave a church, or just drop out when we feel that we are not "holy and without fault." We might see ourselves as imperfect and unworthy, choosing to avoid our bridegroom, Jesus.

Maybe if Jennifer had sat down with John and discussed her fears and insecurities; maybe if we would sit down with Jesus and do the same, the outcome would be different. Jesus would tell us, *"I have offered one sacrifice for all sins forever, and I have perfected all believers forever by that offering. There is no more need for sin offerings because I will remember your sins no more." (My paraphrase from Hebrews 10:12-18)*

In short, as a believer in Christ you are perfect. Your behavior might need some work, but in you, God sees only the perfection of Jesus. All of my "self" esteem has to go. Jesus will replace it with God esteem—how He sees me, who He says I am, and what He says I can accomplish. In Christ, I am accepted, significant, and holy.

The second problem with Jennifer Wilbanks was a lack of concern for others.

One news account read, "The night she disappeared, she withdrew $40.00 with her ATM card. She didn't dare use her card after that because she feared her mother would be able to track her down." Jennifer wasn't concerned about her fiancé, her mother, the wedding guests, the volunteers searching for her, the police, fire, and emergency personnel, her church family or her friends.

Lots of Christians run from Jesus and don't want to be tracked down. They aren't thinking about what their rebellion does to themselves, their families, or the church.

But our bridegroom, Jesus, will never stop loving us. Once we are born again His presence lives within us in the person of the Holy Spirit.

The Spirit of God, who raised Jesus from the dead, lives in you. (Romans 8:11 NLT)

Trying to run from Him is like trying to run away from our blood vessels. Wherever we go, mentally or physically, there He is. The Holy Spirit works inside to turn our hearts back to God the Father—always. That's because we are His beloved children.

As soon as we quit running, all of our relationships improve. Those we tried to avoid suddenly become important again. We find that we have real friends and not just acquaintances. We rediscover the amazing grace and love God has for us.

The third problem with Jennifer Wilbanks was apparently an unwillingness to break with the past and make a full commitment to her bridegroom.

This is the flaw of the double-minded.

… a person with divided loyalty is as unsettled as a wave of the sea that is blown and tossed by the wind. Such people should not expect to receive anything from the Lord. Their loyalty is divided between God and the world, and they are unstable in everything they do. (James 1:6-8 NLT)

Doubt makes us unstable and unable to make commitments. Jennifer Wilbanks had been engaged before and had broken that engagement. While engaged to John Mason she kept a text message on her cell phone from her previous fiancé that read, "I love you." For believers, that's like going back to a law-based religious system after being betrothed to a new husband, Christ.

When we join with Jesus as His bride, we must erase all the messages from our former lovers—the world, the flesh, and the devil. Otherwise, we may think, "Did I make the right decision; am I missing out on some fun; what if I just went back for a little while?" Those are the thoughts of the double-minded, the unstable thoughts of the uncommitted, and the uncertainty of those who will not receive anything from the Lord.

Joshua said it well, *"So honor the LORD and serve him wholeheartedly. Put away forever the idols your ancestors worshiped when they lived beyond the Euphrates River and in Egypt. Serve* the LORD alone. But if you are unwilling to serve the LORD, then choose today whom you will serve. Would you prefer the gods your ancestors served beyond the Euphrates?

Or will it be the gods of the Amorites in whose land you now live? But **as for me and my family, we will serve the LORD**." *(Joshua 24:14-15 NLT)*

Let's decide not to be a runaway bride. We have Holy Spirit power to reject fear of imperfection, selfishness, and doubtful commitment. Besides, He said He will never run away from us.

"I will never fail you. I will never abandon you." (Hebrews 13:5 NLT)

Isn't it great that our spiritual wedding vows do not include the words, "'Til death do us part?" In Christ death has been conquered, and His vow to us is, "Not even death can separate you from My love. We will be together for eternity!" *(See Romans 8:38)*

He Makes All Things New

We spend a lot of time making New Year's resolutions that have no hope of making any one of us a new person for the New Year. The truth is we are simply imposing new *laws* upon ourselves. We are working on behavior modification, while God is working on inner transformation which will always change our behavior for the better. Godly behavior changes take place from the inside out.

The LORD doesn't see things the way you see them. People judge by outward appearance, but the LORD looks at the heart. (1Samuel 16:7 NLT)

Even though on the outside it often looks like things are falling apart on us, on the inside, where God is making new life, not a day goes by without his unfolding grace. (2Corinthians 4:16 NLT)

In the Old Testament God prophesied about the new things He would be doing. In *Isaiah 43* He said, "I will do a new thing," and in *Ezekiel 36* He promised a new heart and new spirit for those who would follow Him.

The fulfillment of hundreds of prophecies culminates at the cross of Christ in a New Covenant of grace, which gives us a new perspective on Scripture. We have new eyes to see, new ears to hear, a new mind and heart to understand the finished work of Christ on the cross.

The old written covenant ends in death; but under the new covenant, the Spirit gives life. (2Corinthians 3:6 NLT)

For believers, the old has passed away and all things have become new. As we read the New Covenant we discover how new it really is: a new nature (His), the new wine (not religion), the new teaching of grace, new birth, new life, a new way of the spirit, a new creation, a new commandment of love, a new song, and much more.

The ultimate future of all believers is also full of new things: a new body, the new Jerusalem, new heavens and new earth, a new name—He makes all things new.

Under grace, we are free from the demands and requirements of the law of Moses and denominational rules and regulations. But wait! There's more to this new covenant of grace. Not only are we free from the *law* of Moses, but we are also free from Moses. This came as a revelation one day as I considered the way so many churches operate.

Moses went up Mount Sinai and met with God who gave him the Ten Commandments. It was a dramatic event.

When the people heard the thunder and the loud blast of the ram's horn, and when they saw the flashes of lightning and the smoke billowing from the mountain, they stood at a distance, trembling with fear. And they said to Moses, "You speak to us, and we will listen. But don't let God speak directly to us, or we will die!" (Exodus 20:18-19 NLT)

The Old Testament of law required that Moses and the prophets bring God's word to the people. Under the New Covenant of grace, we can hear directly from God Himself. We don't need someone to hear from God for us and then pass it on. We are free from Moses!

…you have received the Holy Spirit [the anointing from Him] and he lives within you, so you don't need anyone to teach you what is true. For the Spirit [the anointing] teaches you everything you need to know, and what he teaches is true—it is not a lie. (1John 2:27 NLT)

This is part of our freedom in Christ. If we are overly dependent on a pastor, teacher, author, speaker, or blogger for our understanding of God's Word, we are not as free as we could be.

You have been believers so long now that you ought to be teaching others. (Hebrews 5:12 NLT)

… the Holy Spirit—he will teach you everything … (John 14:26 NLT)

… you have only one teacher, and all of you are equal as brothers and sisters. … you have only one teacher, the Messiah. The greatest among you must be a servant. But those who exalt themselves will be humbled, and those who humble themselves will be exalted. (Matthew 23:8-12 NLT)

Multitudes of Christians are more focused on listening to their favorite pastor/teachers than they are on listening to the Holy Spirit. They are more focused on reading books by their favorite Christian authors than they are on reading God's word.

However, we still need the apostles, prophets, evangelists, pastors and teachers. These are necessary ministry gifts to the Church. They are here to build up and equip people, to teach believers to feed themselves from the Word, to do ministry, and to make disciples. *(See Ephesians 4:11-12)*

These equipping ministries can lead us to the green pasture and still water of the scripture. They can describe it, explain it, and promote its benefits. But the Holy Spirit teaches us through *revelation*, which is much more powerful that any sermon, book, or blog post. The grace of God is *revealed*, not just spoken or read. It doesn't transform our lives until it becomes a revelation, and only the Holy Spirit can make that happen.

The Holy Spirit constantly refreshes and strengthens us.

… we never give up. Though our bodies are dying, our spirits are being renewed every day. (2 Corinthians 4:16 NLT)

He has given me a new song to sing, a hymn of praise to our God. (Psalm 40:3 NLT)

God gave us this new song, not man. What does it mean to sing a new song? There is an expression we use, "After that happened, *he changed his tune.*" And after each new revelation, we will change our tune!

What comes out of our mouths, out of our lives, and through our example will be different. The difference comes about because of our new nature. This new song communicates to the world that we are new creatures, filled with the presence and power of God. We have a new name given by God Himself; and the Gospel of grace, the good news, is for *all* people who will receive it.

I'm not suggesting that you abandon your favorite pastors, teachers, and authors. But test everything you hear or read according to the word of God and let the Holy Spirit bring revelation. Work through tough questions with mature believers who are doing the same.

However, I am suggesting that you abandon obsolete religious ideas and non-biblical denominational demands. Determine to follow Jesus instead of man-made tradition. Embrace the true freedom we have in Christ through His Gospel of grace. It will be life to your soul and health to your bones!

Are You "Second?"

Many churches give out rubber bracelets with reminder messages on them. A friend of mine once wore one with the inscription, *I Am Second*. He told me it means that I must put others before myself. Others say since God is "first" we must be "second." Still others claim it means that as soon as I've been saved God puts me in second place because His first priority is for the unsaved.

I understand what they are saying, and it may sound spiritual, but to me, they all transmit a distorted message of the true Gospel. From the perspective of God's grace, I can't accept being second. I recall the scripture that promises, *"...as He (Jesus) is, so are we in this world. (1John 4:17 NKJV)* Is Jesus "second" with God? If not, then I am not second, either.

In addition, the Bible tells us that believers have been born into God's family, that we are His children. How would you feel if your parent came to you and said, "You're second." I know how I'd feel. I'd feel second-rate.

The church often promotes this idea of our being "second" through its emphasis on the Ten Commandments and other rules and regulations in the law and in the church. My inability to obey, my failures, and my shortcomings all contribute to the idea that I truly am second-rate.

The scriptures tell us that the law is designed to show people their inability to make themselves righteous, and then points them to the only One who can make them righteous—Jesus Christ.

Sin is no longer your master, for you no longer live under the requirements of the law. Instead, you live under the freedom of God's grace. (Romans 6:14 NLT)

Study that verse again. This tells us clearly that the requirements of the law make sin our master. So, following the law is useless for righteousness. The only way out of this slavery, out of condemnation, is through God's grace revealed in Jesus Christ.

So now there is no condemnation for those who belong to Christ Jesus. (Romans 8:1 NLT)

Every believer can say, "That's true because I am filled with the Holy Spirit of God. I am a partaker of the divine nature, the very nature of Jesus Himself. He has given me His life, and His life is free from all condemnation."

No, I am not second with God and neither are you. God does not place any of His children in a pecking order or rank. Jesus Christ is Lord; He has the preeminence. He is the firstborn, but He is not "first" and we are not "second." We are one with Him and He is one with us as we are being transformed into His image.

We are God's chosen children and heirs to the same inheritance as Christ Himself. We are seen by God as being "in Christ." We consider others ahead of ourselves because we love and we serve others before we are served because we have the nature of Christ. So, we are not "second" in any sense of the word. We are His.

Batteries Not Included

Perhaps you can remember opening an electronic toy that promised lots of action and marvels. The instruction book told of all the wonderful things this product was able to do. You pushed the buttons, flipped the switches, turned the knobs and waited for the excitement to begin.

But nothing happened. Promises unfulfilled. Expectations crushed. Your frustration grew as you did everything the book said with no result, certain that it was defective. Then you saw it. The fine print on the cover, "Batteries Not Included."

Religion is like that because it does not come with batteries. It has no power. It does come in many forms, each with a detailed instruction book full of regulations and requirements. As we energetically try to follow them all, we still end up with unfulfilled promises, crushed expectations, and growing frustration. Even the Bible produces the same failed result when approached as a book of rules. It doesn't work. The Bible even tells us why it doesn't work.

The apostle Paul said extremely difficult times were coming. People would love themselves more than God and would adopt many ungodly attitudes *(See 2Timothy 3:1-4)*. He concludes this way, *"They will act religious, but they will reject the power that could make them godly."* (2Timothy 3:5 NLT) In another translation it reads, "[they will have] *a form of godliness but denying its power."* (Ibid. NKJV)

Things made to operate with batteries won't function without them. They need power. We were made to operate with God's power and we can't function properly without it. Chewing on a Duracell won't do it, but receiving the fullness of God's grace in Jesus Christ will.

We could even say, "Jesus Christ comes with power connected." He's not a toy or a gadget and we can't make Him perform by pushing His buttons. But when we receive Jesus Christ as Savior, all the power of almighty God comes into us in the person of the Holy Spirit. The Greek word for power is *dunamis* (our word is "dynamite") which appears more than one hundred times in the New Covenant. Paul often said, in effect, "I depend on *His* power, not mine." *(See 1Corinthians 15:10 and Colossians 1:28-29)*

Jesus said, *"... You will receive power when the Holy Spirit comes upon you." (Acts 1:8 NLT)* If you are born again, you have the power of the Holy Spirit within you—the same Spirit who raised Jesus from the dead. *(See Romans 8:11)*

Stephen was an ordinary person—just like you and me—who by faith operated in the power of God's grace.

Stephen, a man full of God's grace and power, performed amazing miracles and signs among the people. (Acts 6:8 NLT)

Stephen wasn't one of the apostles. He was just a church member who took Jesus at His word. Be assured, all believers are full of the same grace and power. The problem is we've often been taught that we can't expect the same miracles, signs, and lifestyle today. Why not? Perhaps we don't *believe!*

A demon possessed boy was brought to Jesus and his father said, *"Help us if you can." "What do you mean, 'If I can'?" Jesus asked. "Anything is possible if a person believes." (Mark 9:22-23 NLT)*

Not only does this power make it possible for us to work miracles in Jesus' name, but it gives us the power to live righteous lives.

God is working in you, giving you the desire and the power to do what pleases him. (Philippians 2:13 NLT)

The Pharisees in Jesus' day had religion, but they had no power. The Jewish law revealed the perfection of God, but it had no power.

So it is clear that no one can be made right with God by trying to keep the law. (Galatians 3:11 NLT) Religion and law can't make us good—they can only make us guilty. A bathroom scale can't make us slim—it can only tell us we're overweight!

When by grace through faith we are born again into God's family, all our sin is washed away and we are declared good and not guilty for life. All religious laws and obligations—including those found in denominations today—have been fulfilled and made obsolete in Christ. *(See Romans 10:4; Hebrews 8:13)*

Here's the origin of the word, "religion:"

The prefix *re* means to repeat, to do again (as in *rebuild*).

The Latin word *ligare* means to tie, bind.

"Religion," then, is "repeated bondage." An early definition of religion was, "A state of life *bound* by monastic vows."

But we now have God living in us to direct and empower our lives. We no longer need a powerless set of external regulations to guide us. We have Him, in us in person, and we are full of His grace and power.

Jesus promised freedom from a demanding existence of repeated bondage:

"If you abide in My word, you are My disciples indeed. And you shall know the truth, and the truth shall make you free." Therefore if the Son makes you free, you shall be free indeed. (John 8:31-32, 36 NKJV)

Religion: Batteries are not included—no power.

Grace in Christ: Hardwired directly to the source of power—God Himself. This is you in Christ!

"Bye-bye, Stubborn Belly Fat!"

Marie Osmond has been a celebrity endorser of the popular weight-loss program, *Nutri System*. At the time I'm writing this, the television commercials have her saying, "Bye-bye, stubborn belly fat!" This is very effective because those of us who have a bit extra in the middle can relate to how hard it is to get rid of it.

Now, I'm not going to get deep into the medical issues of belly fat but bear with me for just a few sentences. I will make a spiritual connection.

Belly fat, also known as *visceral* fat, is the most harmful fat in our bodies. It's linked to many diseases and medical conditions. These fat cells produce excessive hormones and toxins that attack the vital organs in the abdomen. Belly fat is also extremely difficult to eliminate.

That said, you might be wondering what that has to do with spiritual health. I am convinced that many, many Christians have religious belly fat. The church often feeds its members with unhealthy spiritual food that produces useless spiritual fat. That, in turn, produces spiritual toxins that reduce spiritual vitality and effectiveness.

Unhealthy spiritual food is concocted in religious kitchens. You take one cup of Old Testament law, one cup of denominational rules, two cups of self-effort, and pour in just enough grace to make the mixture somewhat palatable. Just as certain foods should not be eaten together for health reasons, a mixture like this, legalism and grace, produces religious fat. That fat releases toxins of confusion, fear, bondage, and unfruitfulness.

The Bible warns against this mixture many times. There is no place for it in the Gospel of grace. Grace teaches that believers are free from all external religious demands because our lives are now under the internal leadership of the Holy Spirit. It also teaches us that once we are born again nothing we ever say or do will affect our family relationship with God.

This is pretty clear in scripture:

Sin is no longer your master, for you no longer live under the requirements of the law. Instead, you live under the freedom of God's grace. **(Romans 6:14 NLT)**

So Christ has truly set us free. Now make sure that you stay free, and don't get tied up again in slavery to the law. (Galatians 5:1 NLT)

For Christ himself has brought peace to us. He united Jews and Gentiles into one people when, in his own body on the cross, he broke down the wall of hostility that separated us. He did this by ending the system of law with its commandments and regulations. (Ephesians 2:14-15 NLT)

Obviously, freedom means that no system of rules and regulations, scriptural or denominational, has any hold on or power over believers. We now depend on the grace of God to teach us how to live in a Godly manner.

… the grace of God that brings salvation has appeared to all men, teaching us that, denying ungodliness and worldly lusts, we should live soberly, righteously, and godly in the present age… **(Titus 2:11-12 NKJV)**

After we are born again, the problem of spiritual belly fat follows us into our new life in Christ. Religious training, for multitudes of believers, is useless weight we carry. It has no value once we are born again, but we are deeply indoctrinated by what we have been taught in our religious systems. Just like physical belly fat, it's very difficult to get rid of.

To truly come out from under legalism and into grace requires a revelation from God and a revolution in our thinking.

Don't copy the behavior and customs of this world, but let God transform you into a new person by changing the way you think. (Romans 12:2 NLT)

When we realize, in our minds, that we have been perfected forever in Christ, the whole perspective of our lives will change. The religious belly fat starts to melt away. We feel lighter and experience inner peace no matter what this life throws our way. Jesus promised peace to those who have faith in His victory over the enemy's strategy to overcome us with fear, discouragement, and unbelief.

Jesus said, *"I have told you all this so that you may have peace in me. Here on earth you will have many trials and sorrows. But take heart, because I have overcome the world." (John 16:33 NLT)*

So how do we lose this unhealthy religious belly fat? In much the same way we lose it from our round middles (if you suffer from a round middle, that is).

1. **Diet**. Eat a healthy spiritual diet, free from laws and demands. Pure grace—Jesus— is a perfect food. We partake of His divine nature. We digest His Word to nourish us. We eat from the Tree of Life.
2. **Exercise.** Exercise is any activity prompted by the Holy Spirit within us. We are not led into action by our own ideas or the ideas of other well-meaning people. God Himself has the plan, and He reveals it to us through His Spirit and His Word.
3. **Rest.** So many people in the institutional church are always in a flurry of activity, busy-busy-busy. We're maintaining buildings, solving staff problems, managing programs, raising money, arranging special events, and so much more. The Bible does not promote that kind of spiritual lifestyle. God promised us rest in Him. Relax. Be about the Father's business. Go at His pace. Trust me—you will have plenty to do!

4. **Avoid stress.** This, of course, is accomplished by realizing how secure we are in Christ. We worry that we are offending God, disappointing Him, causing Him to be angry with us because we make mistakes and miss the mark so often. He can't be disappointed with us because He knew in advance that we would foul things up. He does not hold our sins against us. He loves us with a perfect love, which eliminates fear. He is not focused on eliminating our sin, but on developing our righteousness (which, in turn, eliminates sin).

Grace, through Jesus Christ, is God's fat-burning diet and exercise program. The more grace we take in, the more religious belly fat we lose. That's really good, healthy news!

Burned!

The conversation went like this—a true personal story:

Officer: "Do you know why I stopped you?"
Me: "I suppose because of the School Zone speed limit?"
Officer: "Didn't you see me parked there?"
Me: "Yes."
Officer: "Then why didn't you slow down?"
Me: "Well, I did put on my brakes."
Officer: "But you didn't slow down."
Me: "I did put on my brakes."
Officer: (Sigh)

Can you tell I was flustered? Then came the look from the officer. It was one of *those* looks. You know, the kind that cuts through all the fakery. Out came the ticket book. "License and registration, please." Shortly he handed me the completed ticket, to the tune of $120.00, and as he walked away I muttered a lame, "I'm sorry." I really was sorry—for a lot of reasons.

Afterward, I thought of all kinds of things to say, such as, "There aren't any blinking yellow lights to warn about the school zone." Or how about this: "I don't usually drive home this way, and I'm not familiar with the area." Surely that would have worked better. Yeah, right. I still would have gotten the look—and the ticket.

Our lives on this earth consist of driving from place to place, doing this and that, filling the time we have with various jobs, activities, projects, and relationships.

For followers of Jesus Christ, there will come a time when we will be pulled over and stopped—when we die—and have to face Him. I don't know exactly how the conversation will go, but the Bible does tell us that there will be one.

For we must all stand before Christ to be judged. We will each receive whatever we deserve for the good or evil we have done in this earthly body. (2Corinthians 5:10 NLT)

The good news in this is that His attitude will not be one of anger, disappointment, or condemnation.

So now there is no condemnation for those who belong to Christ Jesus. (Romans 8:1 NLT)

He will, however, test the things we have done—the Bible calls them "works"—to determine whether they are valuable or worthless. Paul tells us that living our lives is like building a house, where the foundation of our lives is to be Jesus Christ. *(See 1Corinthians 3:11-15)*

On that foundation, we build our lives with our choice of materials: gold, silver, precious stones, wood, hay, or straw. Then, when Jesus meets us at His judgment seat, our born-again life's work will be tested by fire to see what will survive. Even if our works are burned up, He says, we will still be saved, but as though we passed through a wall of fire.

Obviously, the wood, hay, and straw will turn to ashes, but the gold, silver and precious stones will survive. It's pretty evident we should be wise and build our lives with really good, God-approved materials that will survive the fiery testing.

But what is the specific source of the fire? I believe we find it in the book of Revelation where the heavenly Jesus—He who stands in judgment—is described. Part of that description reads like this:

His head and hair were white like wool, as white as snow, and His eyes like a flame of fire. (Rev.1:14)

And when speaking to the church in Thyatira, Jesus said, *"This is the message from the Son of God, whose eyes are like flames of fire." (Revelation 2:18 NLT).*

We can trust the fact that His ability to see is infinitely greater than Superman's X-ray vision. His fiery gaze will burn through all the hypocrisy, the false beliefs, the selfishness, the worldliness, and everything else in our lives that was built of wood, hay, and straw.

Nothing remains hidden or secret from Jesus' view, as he said, *"… everything that is hidden will eventually be brought into the open, and every secret will be brought to light."* (Mark 4:22 NLT) And Paul echoes the same promise, *"Nothing in all creation is hidden from God. Everything is naked and exposed before his eyes, and he is the one to whom we are accountable. (Hebrews 4:13 NLT)*

What's the difference between being "nude" and being "naked?" Well, you're "nude" in the shower at home, but you're "naked" if you run out into Times Square with no clothes on. In other words, you can't hide anything from God, nor can you hide anything that He wants to make known to everyone.

Remember the ticket I got? I sat there in the car while the officer wrote out the ticket. During that time, which felt like about nine hours, a number of elementary school children walked by on their way to school and stared at me. Some smiled a knowing smile. Others pointed and giggled. I felt naked and exposed, my sin visible to the whole world. I remember that more than the sting of the hefty fine.

Thank God for His grace. He will never condemn us for our mistakes and poor choice of building materials. But there are consequences for our choices. *If the work survives, that builder will receive a reward. But if the work is burned up, the builder will suffer great loss. The builder will be saved, but like someone barely escaping through a wall of flames. (1Corinthians 3:14-15 NLT)*

I'm determined to build with the good stuff—the materials that will last for eternity. *(v.14)* Otherwise, I may enter heaven looking like a crispy critter! *(v.15)*

Chalkboard Salvation

Some people teach what I call, "chalkboard salvation." This means that when you're born again God writes your name on His chalkboard. If you sin or do some other ungodly activity, He erases your name. If you repent, He writes it in again. This goes on, over and over again, until either you die with your name written (heaven) or with your name erased (hell), or God runs out of chalk and gives up on you. This is the "you can lose your salvation" message, and it has many variations.

My personal conviction is that once we are born again and made alive in Christ there are no means by which we can lose or reject our salvation. To say otherwise undermines the doctrine of regeneration—being born again—and being united with Christ. The debate between these two positions will go on until Jesus comes, but let me share why I trust in "eternal security."

Every scripture that *sounds* like we might be able to lose or reject our salvation needs to be interpreted from the perspective of God's grace, or we end up with more than one Gospel. The church today is divided and has several different "gospels" about the extent of our security in Christ.

In considering this issue, the main question to ask is, "What takes place in my life when I'm born again?" Here's a list of some of the changes we believers have experienced.

We are united with Christ in His death, burial, resurrection, and ascension and are seated with Him on God's throne. *(See Romans 6:2-4; Ephesians 2:5-7)*

We are united with Christ since God has placed His Holy Spirit in us as His temple. *(See Romans 7:4; 1Corinthians 6:19)*

Our real life is hidden with Christ in God and He lives in us. *(See Colossians 3:1-3; Galatians 2:20)*

We are born of "incorruptible seed," which means our new lives will last forever. *(See 1Peter 1:23)*

We are born into God's family as His children and filled with His Holy Spirit. *(See 1John 5:1; Romans 8:15)*

Christ Himself was placed in us; His future is our future, His life is our life, we share in His glory. *(See Colossians 1:27)*

We will never be condemned for our sins and have already moved from death into eternal life. *(See John 5:24)*

We are blessed with all spiritual blessings because we are united with Christ. *(See Ephesians 1:3)*

We have been set free from all condemnation. *(See Romans 8:1; John 5:24)*

We have been made right with God and therefore we have peace with God. *(See 2Corinthians 5:21; Romans 5:1)*

We have been made holy, set apart to God. *(See 1Corinthians 1:2)*

We have been made perfectly righteous. *(See 2Corinthians 5:21)*

Each of us is a new person and all things have been made new. *(See 2Corinthians 5:17)*

We are sealed, identified with the Holy Spirit. *(See Ephesians 1:13)*

We are a temple, a dwelling place of God's Holy Spirit. *(See 1Corinthians 6:19)*

We have been made complete in Christ. *(See Colossians 2:9-10)*

We have been given a new nature—God's perfect nature, righteous and holy. *(See Ephesians 4:23-24)*

We have been made the same as Christ in spiritual essence. *(See 1John 4:17)*

We have been made perfect forever. *(See Hebrews 10:14)*

So, in order for us to lose or reject salvation, God would have to erase everything we've mentioned above—and more—that was accomplished in us when we were saved. Then to be saved again, He would have to reinstate them. We're back to chalkboard salvation.

But God is once-for-all. As Jesus said from the cross, *"It is finished."* And you can say of your salvation, "It is finished, complete, permanent!"

The key is that we have been spiritually united with Christ. We became one with Him and became *as* Him. The power of this is that Christ has an indestructible life. It is impossible for Christ to ever die again *(See Romans 6:9)*, and so it is impossible for us to die again *(See Romans 6:11)*. Our flesh can die, but the real person we are in Christ can never die.

When Jesus spoke with Nicodemus, the Pharisee, in *John 3*, Nicodemus understood the finality of being born. Indeed, once a person is born, he cannot go back into the womb and be born again. And once a person is spiritually born again, he cannot go back to his previous state of being dead in his sins. Christ's life in us has become our guarantee of eternal salvation.

What about the scriptures that *seem* to warn that a believer can lose salvation? I searched the New Testament for instances where the words "salvation," "save" or "saved" are used to describe being born again and being changed in the ways mentioned above. I stopped when I got to more than fifty instances. These words and this concept were used consistently by the New Testament writers.

However, not once do we find these words used to indicate that salvation can be lost. If it were possible for this very serious event to happen, it seems to me that the writers would make it crystal clear by saying, in effect, "If you do this you will lose your salvation."

All the scriptural arguments I've read to "prove" you can lose your salvation sound to me like reasoning that is intent on rejecting the full extent of God's grace. It's almost as if they are saying, "Believers need the threat of hell to keep them from sinning." Or, "This sounds too good to be true, so there must be a limit to God's grace."

There is no limit to His grace—unless, of course, you return to self-righteous legalism. In that case, you don't lose your salvation, but you do lose a measure of the freedom and security that grace promises for our earthly lives.

*Jesus is the one who **guarantees** this better covenant with God. There were many priests under the old system, for death prevented them from remaining in office. But because Jesus lives **forever**, his priesthood lasts **forever**. Therefore he is able, once and **forever**, to save [to the uttermost*] those who come to God through him. He lives **forever** to intercede with God on their behalf. (Hebrews 7:22-25 NLT) (*NKJV)*

We can rest in our security in Christ. It is something that will encourage and empower us to behave outwardly according to our new inner nature in Christ. Of course, God doesn't use a chalkboard. When we are born again, He writes our names in the Lamb's Book of Life—with a permanent marker.

Welcome To the Complaint Department:

Yesterday Was The Deadline For All Complaints

The new monk was given guidelines for the vow of silence. "You're allowed two words per year," said the bishop. After the first year, he told the bishop, "Food bad." After the second year, he told the bishop, "Bed hard." After the third year, he told the bishop, "I quit." The bishop replied, "I'm not surprised. You've done nothing but complain since you got here."

Complaining is certainly not part of the fruit of the Spirit and, in fact, undermines the love, peace, joy, and patience that come from the Spirit. For the Christian, complaining is debilitating personally and only serves to damage our example to the world. The word translated "complainer" means literally one who is discontented and openly releases frustration. Who would be attracted to a Christian group whose members are dissatisfied with life and who continually grumble and complain?

Clearly, as believers, we are challenged not to grumble or complain.

Do everything without complaining and arguing, so that no one can criticize you. Live clean, innocent lives as children of God, shining like bright lights in a world full of crooked and perverse people. (Philippians 2:14-15 NLT)

If we grumble and complain, it shows how worldly we still are. *(See James 4:1-3)* Complaints come from unfulfilled desires, which lead to jealousy, envy, and quarreling. The foundation of complaining is unbelief. We complain when we don't really believe the promises of God; we blame Him for our problems; we doubt He will help us; we think He has abandoned us, and more.

In the New Covenant God uses the example of the Israelites wandering in the wilderness to warn us about complaining.

And don't grumble as some of them did, and then were destroyed by the angel of death. (1Corinthians 10:6-10 NLT)

God's grace won't allow a complaining believer to be destroyed by the angel of death, but His concern for the well-being of His children motivates Him to give stern warnings. Complaining definitely is something we should avoid, and here's how we do it:

Complaining's Cure, Part 1: Gratitude

In the book, *Springs In The Valley*, Mrs. Charles Cowman tells the parable of a man who found a barn which contained the seeds that Satan sows into the human heart. The seeds of complaining were quite numerous, and he learned that these seeds could be made to grow almost anywhere.

When Satan was questioned, he reluctantly admitted that there was one place where he could never get them to grow. "And where is that?" asked the man. Sadly, Satan replied, "In the heart of a grateful man."

And let the peace that comes from Christ rule in your hearts. For as members of one body you are called to live in peace. And always be thankful. (Colossians 3:15 NLT)

Be thankful in all circumstances, for this is God's will for you who belong to Christ Jesus. (1Thessalonians 5:18 NLT)

What God wants us to do is, as the old song says, *"Count your blessings, name them one by one; count your blessings, see what God has done."* This is not just a cute saying, it is one part of the cure for a complaining spirit. Being thankful brings His peace, and the will of God is that we be at peace. He wants peace to rule in our hearts, particularly in the midst of challenging or painful circumstances.

Complaining's Cure, Part 2: Contentment

Some years ago, Charles Schulz pictured Charlie Brown bringing out Snoopy's dinner on Thanksgiving Day, but it was just his usual dog food in a bowl. Snoopy took one look at the dog food and said, "This isn't fair. The rest of the world is eating turkey with all the trimmings and all I get is dog food. Why? Because I'm a dog, so all I get is dog food?" He stood there and stared at his dog food for a moment, and then he said, "I guess it could be worse. I could be a turkey."

Let your conduct be without covetousness; be content with such things as you have. For He Himself has said, "I will never leave you nor forsake you." (Hebrews 13:5 NKJV)

I have learned in whatever state I am, to be content… (Philippians 4:11 NKJV)

Now godliness with contentment is great gain. For we brought nothing into this world, and it is certain we can carry nothing out. And having food and clothing, with these we shall be content. (1 Timothy 6:6-8 NKJV)

God has given us everything we need for life and godliness. *(See 2Peter 1:3)* God has promised to provide everything we need according to His riches in glory. *(See Philippians 4:19)* He has promised to take the difficult times of life and create something good for us. *(See Romans 8:28)* These undeserved benefits of His grace and so many more are ample cause for thanksgiving and contentment.

When we truly understand the riches of God's grace, our joy and peace will abound. People will wonder how we can consistently be that way, particularly when facing difficult times. What an opportunity to share God's grace!

If yesterday was the day before I was born again, then yesterday was truly the deadline for all complaints.

From One Clay Pot to Another

A common deception among Christians is that somehow people should admire us and our goodness because we have been born again and have the image of Jesus. But Paul warns against this when he writes, *"… we have this treasure in earthen vessels, [clay pots] that the excellence of the power may be of God and not of us." (2Corinthians 4:7 NKJV)*

Man was made to be a container, not a creator, originator, or a self-actualized person. Man was created to contain God, and only when he does that does he function normally by expressing God's character and fulfilling God's plan. When we are born again we contain the Holy Spirit, the presence of God.

Believers are described as clay pots with the treasure inside. The container is not the treasure and never will be. Clay is humble material. Our flesh is humble material. There is no glory in the clay or the flesh, only in what they contain. And if what they contain cannot be seen, tasted, or heard, then nothing of real value can be produced. Therefore, our pots are to be transparent, which allows the light we contain to be seen in the darkness around us. Then the focus is not on us, but on Christ in us.

The Bible uses other images, for example, a *temple*, and a *branch*, to express this same container concept. Each believer is a *temple* of the Holy Spirit.

Don't you realize that your body is the temple of the Holy Spirit, who lives in you and was given to you by God? You do not belong to yourself, for God bought you with a high price. So you must honor God with your body. (1Corinthians 6:19-20 NLT)

In other words, our physical bodies are holy containers that house the glory of God, His Holy Spirit. The temple is not the glory and is not intended to be. The glory is what's inside the temple.

We might build beautiful, magnificent church buildings with expensive materials and furnishings, adorn them with stained glass windows, and fill them with high definition images, studio quality sound, and professional performances. None of that is the glory. The glory enters the building with the first humble, born-again believer who walks through the door.

In addition, we are described as *branches* that contain the life of Jesus, the vine. Jesus said, *"Abide in Me, and I in you. As the branch cannot bear fruit of itself, unless it abides in the vine, neither can you, unless you abide in Me. "I am the vine, you are the branches. He who abides in Me, and I in him, bears much fruit; for without Me you can do nothing. (John 15:4-5 NKJV)*

The branch on the grapevine cannot produce fruit on its own but is simply a conduit through which the life of the vine flows. Then the fruit on the branch is produced by that life. The branch's function is to hold the fruit as it develops. Believers are branches that provide a conduit for the life of Christ. We then will bear, or hold, the fruit of the Spirit as it develops in our lives.

The presence of God within us is of benefit to us, but it is to be shared liberally with those around us. He is not in us to make *us* look good but to make *Jesus* look good. Since we are all ministers as we travel through our lives, day by day, we can apply to ourselves the encouragement Paul gave to Timothy.

Be an example to all believers in what you say, in the way you live, in your love, your faith, and your purity. (1Timothy 4:12 NLT)

So, from one clay pot to another, or from one see-through saint to another, let me encourage you to let His glory be seen in you. He has equipped us fully and completely to do just that.

By his divine power, God has given us everything we need for living a godly life. (2Peter 1:3a NLT)

How To Handle Difficult People

Are there any difficult people in your life?
Is there anyone in your life who *isn't* difficult?

Don't you wish everyone could be as wonderful as you?

The book of James is a very practical and honest look at the human condition.

Dear brothers and sisters, when troubles [difficult people included] *of any kind come your way, consider it an opportunity for great joy. For you know that when your faith is tested, your endurance has a chance to grow. So let it grow, for when your endurance is fully developed, you will be perfect and complete, needing nothing. (James 1:2-4 NLT)*

Troubles, tests, and trials often come through difficult people. They can be undependable, dishonest, selfish, manipulative, bitter, unimaginative, quarrelsome, disinterested, arrogant, dangerous, or greatly gifted at causing turmoil. Difficult people are often broken people. Something in their lives isn't working right. That means—and I know it's hard to believe—that even you and I could be difficult people occasionally.

Why do we avoid dealing with broken things? Well, it takes too much trouble, time, money, or effort to fix them. Just throw it away and get a new one—a car, toaster oven, outboard motor, computer, whatever. Unfortunately, we might have the same attitude toward broken people—perhaps a husband, wife, child, church member, friend, president, parent, fishing buddy, whoever.

Jesus didn't see difficult people as a pain; he saw them as people in need. When we encounter a difficult person, we might decide we don't like him, don't enjoy her, or don't want to be around him.

But Jesus never had that attitude. James and John were called the "sons of thunder" for their hot-headed attitude, their selfish ambition. In *Mark 10* they asked Jesus, "In your Kingdom, we want to sit in places of honor next to you, one at your right and the other at your left."

Jesus responded, "Do you think you can handle the same extreme level of suffering I'm going to endure?"

They replied, "Absolutely! We sure can!"

Jesus ended with, "Only the Father can assign those positions." Note that He never rejected them or put them down for their arrogance.

And there were so many others. The woman at the well, with five husbands and living in adultery with another man. The Pharisees who were always trying to trap Him and get Him arrested. The would-be disciples who weren't willing to sell out and follow Him. In all cases, Jesus acted with redemption in view. To Him, they all had value, potential, and a future. His aim was to guide them, even if He had to get tough, into a restored relationship with the Father.

Then there's the account of Jesus having dinner with some shady characters, and the Pharisees asked His disciples, "Why does He eat with such nasty sinners?"

When Jesus heard this, he told them, "Healthy people don't need a doctor—sick people do. I have come to call not those who think they are righteous, but those who know they are sinners." (Mark 2:17)

In other words, He came for the difficult ones.

Peter was a hard-headed, pushy, egotistical blowhard who just didn't get it. He wanted a big job in the kingdom, complained about giving up everything for Jesus, sank when he tried to walk on water, directly opposed the will of God prompting Jesus to tell him he was being used by Satan, cut off the ear of one who came to arrest Jesus when Jesus told him not to, abandoned Jesus when

He was crucified, and to save his own skin he even swore he never knew Jesus.

But Jesus always encouraged Peter, sometimes gently and sometimes strongly. Ultimately in *John 21* He fully restored Peter to a right relationship. Peter survived it all and became one of the foundation stones of the early church.

And what about Judas Iscariot, the betrayer? Jesus treated him as one of the others, with redemption in view. Jesus knew all about Judas:

He was a thief—and Jesus made him treasurer.

He was a mocker, a hypocrite, a devil, a traitor—and Jesus washed his feet.

He gave the kiss of betrayal when Jesus was arrested—and Jesus simply said, *"Judas, how can you betray me, the Son of Man, with a kiss?" (Luke 22:48 NLT)*

It looks like Jesus never gave up on Judas. But Judas didn't make it. Zacchaeus, the tax collector, got it. But the rich man who came to Jesus wanting eternal life apparently didn't. People attending church meetings? Some will get it, some won't. The difficult people in our lives? Some will get it, some won't.

We need to pray, "Lord Jesus, help me see these difficult people with *your* eyes, and then help me respond to them with compassion." Sometimes we might have to overturn some tables and use a strong response. Other times we might respond with love and patience. In any case, Paul encourages us to *"… walk worthy of the calling with which you were called, with all lowliness and gentleness, with longsuffering, bearing with one another in love, endeavoring to keep the unity of the Spirit in the bond of peace." (Ephesians 4:1-3 NKJV)*

The goal is always the same—redemption. Jesus died for difficult people and made redemption available to them. If we believe that then we can do as Jesus says, *"Love your enemies! Pray for those who persecute you!* [Let's add here, "Pray for those really difficult people in your life."] *In that way, you will be acting as true children of your Father in heaven." (See Matthew 5:43-48 NLT)*

I do not always handle difficult people well. But I handle them better than I used to. And when strong action is necessary—and it has been on several occasions—my motive is, "Perhaps this will wake them up."

How to handle difficult people? See everyone with Jesus' eyes as someone eligible for healing, as someone with potential, as someone loved and valued by God, as someone on whom God has not given up.

Easy? No way. Worth it? Absolutely!

Simply Forgiven

She walked along the well-worn street, ignoring the condemning glances from those she passed. She was carefully dressed and groomed, but not as meticulously as when she was looking for a man to entertain. Oh, she was looking for a man, but she knew he would not be interested in her in the usual way. She clutched her flask of frankincense tightly, fearful of dropping the fragile container on the stone roadway.

He was nearby. She could sense a growing excitement in the air as she approached the house. A small group of people was standing just off the street, peering into the home's open dining area. She heard the murmur of conversation around the table, the occasional laugh that men laughed when they were sure of themselves. She knew the sound well.

As she approached, her mind filled with the images of many past social gatherings she had attended. However, those were usually private, out of sight of the curious, and under the cover of darkness.

She stopped a few steps away from the group of spectators. Who was she to be this close to powerful religious leaders? She would not be welcome here. In fact, the men in attendance would want to chase her into the street like a stray dog if she got too close. But she knew at least some, particularly one man, would not reject her.

She wished for the cover of darkness, but it was mid-day and she could not hide from prying eyes. She moved ahead slowly behind those watching the dinner party. Rising up on her toes, she gazed into the room. There were many men reclining at the table, served by several young women. She recognized some of the religious leaders from the Temple. They were very high in rank, arrogant and self-assured.

Her eyes surveyed the faces, looking for the one she had come to see. The rumor was that he was here, but she could not tell which one he was. A woman in front of her pushed past her, opening her view of those closest to the street.

Then she saw him, reclining with his feet directly toward her. Slowly, she moved toward him through the group of onlookers. Yes, it was him. As she came closer, her eyes filled with tears. Her boldness increased even as she felt weak and unworthy. Only one woman remained between her and the reclining man she had come to see. She pushed gently past her and stood at his feet.

The tears now began to flow freely as she knelt down, sobbing quietly, her tears falling on his feet. As he felt her tears touch him he gave her his full attention and the room fell silent. The eating and drinking ceased, the serving women stood still, and the only sound was her soft weeping.

Her long hair fell to the sides of his feet and she used it to wipe them gently. He said nothing, but she sensed his love and compassion. Oh, he discerned what kind of woman she was, but he allowed her to express her devotion without interruption. She poured her fragrant oil on his feet and kissed them lightly.

The Pharisee who had invited Jesus stood watching with shock and anger at her boldness. Jesus spoke to him, but she paid little attention to his exact words. He rebuked the host for failing to welcome him properly and commended her for washing his feet with her tears, wiping them with her hair, anointing them with oil, and kissing them with love.

Jesus projected nothing but grace and mercy. There was no rebuke or condemnation in His eyes. She heard him clearly as he spoke directly to her, "Your sins are forgiven." The temple officials were offended and dismayed, but His words washed over her and through her entire being as a refreshing, cleansing flood. She lifted her head and looked into his eyes. He simply said, "Your faith has saved you, go in peace."

She stood, free from all her fear, guilt, shame and condemnation. The tears continued as tears of joy as she walked toward her home and into a new life.

What can we say about such a wonderful story? *(See Luke 7:36-50)* Thank you, Lord, for your grace! Note that there was no sinner's prayer, no laundry list of sins, no questions, demands or requirements of any kind. What we see here is faith expressed in love, believing that Jesus was who He said He was, and that He would save and give new life to anyone who came to Him with true humility. It's not complicated. God's plan of salvation is intentionally simple. His grace is sufficient to save us and keep us, no matter what.

From my experience, forgiveness is the most distorted teaching in the church. The religious message is one of "conditional" forgiveness. It teaches that when we believers sin we must do something (perform) in order to make it right with God. This might consist of asking God to forgive us, or it might be a system of restitution, penance, prayer, ritual or the like. The problem with that belief is that we remain in constant fear and uncertainty. Did I do it right? Did I do enough? Did I remember every single sin? What if I forgot one? What if I die with unforgiven sin?

The other problem is that we're suggesting that the blood of Christ was not sufficient to wash away all sin. We divide sinful behavior into past sin and future sin, but the Bible makes no such distinction. All sin was paid for at the cross. With God, forgiveness is absolutely unconditional for a person who is born again!

This issue deserves serious study. The Holy Spirit is a more effective teacher than any human teacher. And as a born-again child of God, you have the mind of Christ. Listen to the man at the table who still says, "Your faith has saved you, go in peace."

Are You Disillusioned? Good!

Have you ever been disappointed with someone, thinking he was one kind of person and then you suddenly find out he wasn't? Or maybe you had great expectations for a person and she failed to come through. The hurt comes when you experience reality after believing the illusion, hence the term, "dis-illusioned."

The illusions we have about people are often created either by the people themselves or by our own wishful thinking. When the illusion is shattered, we are hurt and call these people hypocrites, or we beat ourselves up over our foolishness.

If we're not careful, we can become cynical, bitter, critical, and severe in our judgment of others. Religious organizations tend to create people who are careful to be good, avoid evil, and obey all the rules to appear holy. But under the surface is often a very different person. Jesus said of the Jewish religious leaders, *"You are like whitewashed tombs—beautiful on the outside but filled on the inside with dead people's bones and all sorts of impurity. (Matthew 23:27 NLT)*

Religion's focus is always on the outward appearance, working hard to control behavior and performance. Man's religion produces only behavior modification, but God's grace produces character transformation.

Jesus knew how to avoid the hurts of disillusionment. John observed, *"… many began to trust in him. But Jesus didn't trust them because he knew human nature. No one needed to tell him what mankind is really like." (John 2:23-25 NLT)*

He was never cynical about people because He had no illusions about them, had no false perceptions or misconceptions. Therefore,

He couldn't be disappointed in them. God's grace helps us see people as they really are, and love them anyway without being cynical or critical.

But wait—doesn't the Bible condemn people's failures? For example, Paul wrote, *"No one is righteous— not even one. No one is truly wise; no one is seeking God. All have turned away; all have become useless. No one does good, not a single one." (Romans 3:10-12 NLT)*

This is not condemnation, but simply the truth. Our reaction to people's failures should not be to avoid, criticize, or be hurt, but rather to nod our heads in understanding. God is saying, "Don't have any illusions about the goodness of people. I sure don't."

Yet Jesus loved people intensely. He accepted the truth about them. He took them just as they were and didn't become jealous, suspicious or bitter. He simply accepted the fact that people are imperfect. He could do that because His confidence was not in people, but in God who could transform them. He trusted in the power of God's grace to sanctify the nastiest sinner, and never gave up hope.

If we love someone but don't understand God's grace, we tend to expect perfection from that person. When that doesn't happen, we become upset and hurt. We are expecting something that a human being can't give. It's something that only God can give.

God's grace gives us the power to love people the same way Jesus does.

[God] *has given us the Holy Spirit to fill our hearts with his love. (Romans 5:5 NLT)*

His grace gives us the power to accept people the same way Jesus Christ does— just as they are.

God showed his great love for us by sending Christ to die for us while we were still sinners. (Romans 5:8 NLT)

No person, except Jesus, can measure up to every expectation. We can expect perfection from Jesus because He is perfect. When someone fails, out of our love for that person we simply trust God's power to make it right and to do it His way.

Let God's love and grace control you through the Holy Spirit, and you are free—free to love everyone as Jesus commanded, free of bitterness, disappointment, and frustration. With Christ, there are no illusions, just the reality of His love which covers a multitude of sins.

The Battle Regarding Divine Healing

I've come to the place in my spiritual life where I resist—not always successfully—the attitude that says I have found the final answer to a question and I'm not willing to consider any opposing views. I'm just not that smart, and I've had to modify my thinking many times over the years.

Divine healing is one of those topics that leads to extremes. At one end we have the extreme faith belief that if healing doesn't come you don't have enough faith, you didn't pray right, you don't really believe in healing, or you have some sin that's in the way. A person can pull out verses of scripture to support that belief.

At the other end is the fatalistic view that whatever will be, will be, and God just doesn't miraculously heal anymore. A person could probably quote scripture for that, too.

In the middle are many mixtures of these two extremes, including the belief is that God causes sickness, or wills people to be sick, or stands idly by and allows them to be sick without helping, or uses sickness to teach people a lesson.

Sickness and disease are definitely not part of God's plan for His children. He does not want His children to suffer, so why do we suffer from these things? I'm not even going to try to answer that one. My position is pretty simple—I will lay hands on, anoint with oil, and pray for the sick, believing in faith that they will recover.

Is anyone among you sick? Let him call for the elders of the church, and let them pray over him, anointing him with oil in the name of the Lord. And the prayer of faith will save the sick, and the Lord will raise him up. (James 5:14-15 NKJV)

I will speak life, challenge disease and death, and encourage them from scripture about the grace, love, and power of God. If they should not recover, I won't condemn myself or anyone else for not having enough faith. I won't try to explain why they weren't healed. If lack of faith is the answer, then just how does a person increase faith? Just how do I believe more? I think I have the answer to that one. I will simply continue to build on my relationship with Christ and grow in my knowledge of Him, just as Paul was doing in *Philippians 3*.

Taking that position helps me when confronted with very difficult questions. For example, in *John 11* we read that Jesus received a report that His friend Lazarus was sick and dying, and yet He didn't go to him to heal him. Lazarus died. We know Jesus can heal from a distance because He did it more than once. In fact, when Jesus heard about Lazarus' death, He made a very unusual statement.

"Lazarus is dead. And for your sakes, I'm glad I wasn't there, for now you will really believe. (John 11:14-15 NLT) What? "I'm glad I wasn't there?"

And so the questions arise: Why didn't He heal Lazarus, and allow him to die? Did He have a greater purpose in mind through raising him from the dead a few days later? Did Jesus abandon His friend Lazarus to sickness and death just to make a point? Is that the way He still operates?

Maybe you have a theological answer, but here's mine: Jesus is Lord. His ways are always full of grace, love, and mercy. He is the resurrection and the life. I'll have to ask Him about it when I see Him.

Here are some other questions people battle over. Whose faith energizes the healing? Is it my faith or the faith of the one who is sick? Is if my fault if someone is not healed, or is it their fault, or is it God who says, "No?" Same answer: Jesus is Lord, and I am not. It's not that I don't care about the answer, but if I try to explain, it only causes confusion.

I have read a lot about divine healing from many educated men and women of God. Authors of books and commentaries have tried to get a handle on it. They don't all agree, and they all have scripture to support their various views. I'd rather point people to Jesus through their struggle, and encourage them to simply trust Him. He does know best and will always do what is right.

To be honest, I'm weary of trying to figure it all out. Jesus is still the healer. He still does miracles. He wants us to be part of the process, and that includes our praying and believing. He doesn't cause sickness any more than a loving earthly father would injure his child to teach him a lesson.

Let me repeat what I said earlier. I will lay hands on, anoint with oil, and pray for the sick, believing in faith that they will recover. I will speak life, challenge disease and death, and encourage them from scripture about the grace, love, and power of God.

So, I'm studying and praying to know Him more and to build a more intimate relationship with Him. That's the same road that Paul traveled. He wanted to know Him intimately, to experience the power of His resurrection, and to have fellowship with Him through the difficulties that come with following Him.

Paul said it clearly, *"I no longer count on my own righteousness through obeying the law; rather, I become righteous through faith in Christ. For God's way of making us right with himself depends on faith. I want to know Christ and experience the mighty power that raised him from the dead. I want to suffer with him, sharing in his death, so that one way or another I will experience the resurrection from the dead!"* (Philippians 3:9-11 NLT)

I invite you to join Paul in his perspective of God's grace and then to see the great things He will accomplish through you. Ultimately, we will all be healed and made whole for eternity in our glorified bodies. *[God] will wipe every tear from their eyes, and there will be no more death or sorrow or crying or pain. All these things are gone forever."* (Revelation 21:4 NLT)

Why Doesn't God DO Something?

Let's say you need God to heal, or to restore, or to provide, or to set free, or to (insert your need here), and nothing is happening.

You've prayed and you've asked, "Where is God? Why doesn't He *do* something? Doesn't He care?"

I'm writing this on a Wednesday after Palm Sunday, the church's celebration of the day when Jesus entered Jerusalem and the people cheered the Messiah. "Hosanna," they yelled, waving palm branches, "Blessed is he who comes in the name of the Lord!" *(See Mark 11:9-10)*

Just a few days later, many of the same people cursed Him and demanded His death on a cross. *(See Mark 15:13-14)* Why the change? Well, He didn't do what they wanted Him to do, what they expected of their Messiah. They wanted Him to use His power to free Israel from bondage to Rome and to restore the throne of King David. Instead, He was arrested and condemned to die.

For the disciples and many others in Jerusalem, the period between Jesus' arrest and His resurrection was filled with anger, frustration, crushed hopes and dreams, fear, and uncertainty. "How could this happen?" they questioned. "We thought He was the answer for Israel. He wouldn't even defend Himself. He certainly had great power, so why didn't He use it? Why didn't God *do* something?!"

Today, many believers in Christ are living between Palm Sunday and the resurrection. They are disappointed in Jesus because He isn't doing what they want Him to do or what they think He should do. Finances. Healing. Relationships. Deliverance from addiction. Job. Children. Ministry. The list of our desires is long, and while most of us won't admit it, we can become disappointed, frustrated, hopeless, fearful, even angry at God.

We may wonder, "Where is He when I need Him?" To answer, we need to go beyond the cross and the disappointment of unfulfilled desire. What's beyond? The resurrection, of course. Jesus' resurrection proves that Jesus has power over death, and power to give life to all those who receive Him. He not only gives life, but He gives *His* life—resurrection life.

Therefore we were buried with Him through baptism into death, that just as Christ was raised from the dead by the glory of the Father, even so we also should walk in newness of life. For if we have been united together in the likeness of His death, certainly we also shall be in the likeness of His resurrection… (Romans 6:4-5 NKJV)

This "newness of life" empowers us to live above all of life's challenges. The Gospel is more than "Jesus died for our sins." It goes on to say, "And He gives us His life in the here and now!"

Yes, we believers now, today, have *His* life; an eternal life that began when we were born again. The term "eternal life" means more than simply "living forever." It means abundant, rich, full, satisfying life in the present. It's a *quality* of life as well as *quantity*.

Once the life of Christ replaces our old life we have no need to prove anything to God. And God has nothing more to prove to us. He has already done it all. We simply live out this new life in total faith and trust.

This new life looks very different from the old life. It changes our behavior, values, speech, interests, attitudes, desires—the whole life is brand new. Every day begins fresh and new, energized with His life in us.

Great is his faithfulness; his mercies begin afresh each day. (Lamentations 3:23 NLT)

Every time we complain that God isn't doing what we want, or what we think He should do, we are living between the cross and the resurrection. By faith we can move into the Holy-Spirit-empowered life we received when we were born again.

Then Paul's well-known scripture becomes real in us.

My old self has been crucified with Christ. It is no longer I who live, but Christ lives in me. So I live in this earthly body by trusting in the Son of God, who loved me and gave himself for me. (Galatians 2:20 NLT)

This is a *new* life, not an old life that has been reconditioned, refurbished, or factory rebuilt. And when we truly grab onto that new life, we will not be crushed by the difficult circumstances of our earthly lives. Our faith in Christ and His love for us empowers us to live above anything that comes our way.

We should receive for ourselves and for the church Paul's prayer for the church at Ephesus:

I pray that your hearts will be flooded with light so that you can understand the confident hope he has given to those he called—his holy people who are his rich and glorious inheritance.

I also pray that you will understand the incredible greatness of God's power for us who believe him. This is the same mighty power that raised Christ from the dead and seated him in the place of honor at God's right hand in the heavenly realms. (Ephesians 1:18-20 NLT)

So, if you are born again, you are a new creation filled with the life of God Himself. If you've prayed and you catch yourself being upset with God's apparent lack of performance, let it be a wake-up call to change focus, trusting that—no matter what—God is at work causing everything to work for the good of you, His child. You are free to live!

Let's Get Those Ducks In A Row

Here's a great quote from Judah Smith, pastor of City Church in Seattle:

"The gospel is good news for everyone, and not just for people who are already good, for those who are self-controlled and disciplined enough to have all their ducks in a row. It's good news for the people who can't even find their ducks. Some of them haven't seen their ducks in years. Their lives are a mess. But they can come to Jesus and find instant help, wholeness, and acceptance."

Can you relate? You think you've got it, then you fail, you sin, you blow it big time. Sometimes we have trouble experiencing born-again life the way the Bible describes it.

- We are new people; old things are gone, all things are new. *(See 2Corinthians 5:17)*
- The new man is righteous and holy. *(See Ephesians 4:24)*
- Jesus became sin so we could be righteous. *(See 2Corinthians 5:21)*

Then we say, "If that's all true, then why do I still do bad stuff? What is going on with me? I should have a neat row of ducks!"

Paul faced the same dilemma. He wrote, *"I don't really understand myself, for I want to do what is right, but I don't do it. Instead, I do what I hate. ... I am not the one doing wrong; it is sin living in me that does it. ... I want to do what is good, but I don't. I don't want to do what is wrong, but I do it anyway. ...I am not really the one doing wrong; it is sin living in me that does it."* (Excerpts from Romans 7:14-20 NLT)

Here, Paul twice says that sin dwells in him. Sin may be *in* us, but it is *not* us. I read somewhere a good illustration of this point, "When I had a kidney stone, I didn't call myself 'Rocky' because the stone wasn't me, it was only in me." There is no sin in our born-again spirit, our true identity which is Christ in us, the hope of glory.

In Christ, you are a holy person who still lives in a human body. Our flesh has the residual effect of the sin that used to be your identity as a person. You *were* a sinner, but no longer!

Since we have been united with him in his death, we will also be raised to life as he was. We know that our old sinful selves were crucified with Christ so that sin might lose its power in our lives. We are no longer slaves to sin. For when we died with Christ we were set free from the power of sin. And since we died with Christ, we know we will also live with him. (Romans 6:5-8 NLT)

By faith, we can now embrace the truth of what it means to live the life He has placed in us. He lives His life *through* us *as* us. *(See Romans 8:11)* We can go on trying to overcome challenges in our own strength (living under the law by our performance), or we can believe and trust in what God has promised us as His children (living under grace according to the finished work of Christ on the cross).

There is a big difference between sin in the Old Testament and sin in the New Covenant; i.e. before the Cross and after the Cross. The general meaning of sin is to "miss the mark," or "fall short."

The Old Testament mark was the Law of Moses; 613 laws plus the commentary and analysis written in the Talmud and Mishna. These provide *external* direction. The New Covenant mark is the life of Christ within us which shows itself outwardly through our obedience to the Holy Spirit. This provides *internal* direction.

Old Covenant sin was a violation of the law of Moses. The remedy was to cover sin with the blood of sacrificed animals. Everything took place externally since God was not *in* people. This practice was never able to take away sin. *(See Hebrews 10:4)*

New Testament sin is choosing our fleshly and worldly desires over the indwelling life of Christ. It shows in our words, attitude, and behavior. It does *not* separate us from God because He is *in* us. It does not require sacrifice because the blood of Christ was the final sacrifice and has taken away, washed away all sin.

The distortion of the Gospel of Grace comes when we view sin from the Old Testament perspective, causing us to live with guilt, fear, doubt, pressure to perform, and the like. This is not freedom. This steals our peace and joy. Jesus came to set us free. Jesus promised that our peace and joy would be full.

For the law of the Spirit of life in Christ Jesus [grace] *has made me free from the law of sin and death* [religion]. *(Romans 8:2 NKJV)*

Believers now live under the spirit of life (grace) and have been made free from the law of sin and death, which represents the flesh, the law, religion, and the power of sin.

Galatians 5:16-22 encourages us to walk in the Spirit and we'll have victory over the flesh.

Hebrews 12:1-2 says to lay aside our old patterns and to live our life looking to Jesus, the One who started us on the faith path and who will see us through to the end.

Colossians 3:1-3 says think about things above, not on the things of the earth because your real life is hidden with Christ in God.

Romans 6:7 says again that when we died with Christ we were set free from sin.

All this and more means that we can confidently believe and trust that sin no longer controls us. It's a matter of focus. Will we focus on our failures, or on Christ's success? We've all proven that to overcome temptation by our willpower doesn't work. What does work is to believe by faith that we are dead to sin, our life is in Christ, and He has given us the victory.

... every child of God defeats this evil world, and we achieve this victory through our faith. (1 John 5:4 NLT)

Our faith comes from God, not from ourselves. We learn who we are in Christ. We learn the full truth about what Jesus accomplished when He said, "It is finished!" By grace, we *are* forgiven, and the grace of God teaches us to avoid worldly desires and to live godly lives *(See Titus 2:11-12)*

Grace is not an excuse to sin, it is the power to help us overcome. We are encouraged to come boldly to God's throne of grace for help. *(See Hebrews 4:16)* The focus is on His ability, not mine. We defeat temptation and do right things because we *want* to, and trust God to empower us by His grace to follow through.

Let's always agree with God as to who we are in Christ. The Spirit of life in Christ speaks life to our soul, the soul energizes the mouth to speak words in agreement with God, and the result is faith and overcoming power.

After Paul lamented about his many failures to do right and avoid wrong, he ends with, *"But thank God! He gives us victory over sin and death through our Lord Jesus Christ." (1 Corinthians 15:57 NLT)*

As a born-again child of God, you are filled with all the power and love of your Father. He works in you to put all your ducks in a row.

God is working in you, giving you the desire and the power to do what pleases him. (Philippians 2:13 NLT)

You Are The Same As Jesus

Don't tune out as you read the title. This chapter may be radical truth for some, but it has the potential to change the way you see yourself forever.

Before you were born again (saved), God knew you. In fact, He not only knew you but also chose you before the foundation of the world. *(See Ephesians 1:4)* You belonged to Him. The devil never owned you; he has never owned anything. He is a thief, and no matter how long a thief keeps stolen property, it never belongs to him. The devil has kidnapped God's creation and lied to them. All creation belongs to God.

The earth is the LORD'S, and all its fullness, The world and those who dwell therein. (Psalm 24:1 NKJV)

You and I were once lost, and you can't be lost unless you once belonged. We simply needed to come home. We needed to recognize that we were lost and then to accept the sacrifice Jesus made for our sin, receive Him as Savior, and exchange our lives for His. In short, we needed to believe and respond to the Gospel.

Once we are found, there is good news about our identity and value.

Love has been perfected among us in this: that we may have boldness in the day of judgment; because as He [Jesus] is, so are we in this world. (1 John 4:17 NKJV)

As Jesus is, so are we as we live in this world. As children of God, we don't need to ask, "Am I accepted by God?" We need only to ask, "Is Jesus accepted by God?" If Jesus is, so are we.

Man-made religion loves to get us focused on ourselves and our behavior, faults, shortcomings, and sin—even our own goodness.

"You're not doing enough," it tells us. "You're not as spiritual as Nancy." "You're going to pay for what you did." "You're so wise and gifted."

However, God wants us focused on Jesus, encouraging us to *"… run with endurance the race that is set before us, looking unto Jesus, the author and finisher of our faith …" (Hebrews 12:1-2 NKJV)*

If Jesus is at the Father's right hand, so are we.
If Jesus is favored by the Father, we are, too.
If Jesus is protected by the Father, He protects us also.
If Jesus is not condemned by the Father, neither are we.

God does not judge us. He judges the perfection and the finished work of His Son. When the Old Testament priest stood at the altar of sacrifice, he represented God. As the worshiper approached the altar with his sacrificial lamb, the priest didn't look at the man, he looked at the lamb. The priest did not ask the man, "How good are you?" but, "How good is your lamb?"

Religion says, "Examine your heart." But grace says, "Examine your lamb—Jesus." As Jesus is, so are we—perfect!

For He made Him who knew no sin to be sin for us, that we might become the righteousness of God in Him. (2Corinthians 5:21 NKJV)

If you are a believer, God holds up Jesus and says, "Look. This is you." Your first inclination may be to respond, "No, that's not me. Jesus is perfect, blameless, powerful, and I'm imperfect, guilty, and weak." Yet God will say, "I appreciate your honesty, but my truth trumps your honesty. You are not seeing yourself as I see you—perfect, blameless, and powerful. Look again."

In the first chapter of his letter, the apostle James shows us that there are two ways for a believer to look into the mirror of the Gospel of grace.

For if you listen to the word and don't obey, it is like glancing at your face in a mirror. You see yourself, walk away, and forget what you look like. But if you look carefully into the perfect law that sets you free, and if you do what it says and don't forget what you heard, then God will bless you for doing it. (James 1:23-25 NLT)

Some believers carelessly look in the mirror of God's Word, see themselves as a new creation in Christ, and then forget what they see and go back to their old lifestyle. Others look carefully, believe they are who God says they are, do *not* forget, and then live out their new life in freedom.

God is never going to change His perception of us. What needs to change is our attitudes and behavior, and that change is something that God's grace gives us the power and desire to do. As we come to know who we are in Christ, we will behave more and more like who we are. We will gradually be formed outwardly to match the nature of Christ within us.

Some folks asked Jesus if they should pay taxes to Caesar. He said, *"Show me a Roman coin. Whose picture and title are stamped on it?" "Caesar's," they replied. "Well then," he said, "give to Caesar what belongs to Caesar, and give to God what belongs to God." (Luke 20:24-25 NLT)*

As a believer, whose image and likeness is stamped on you? It's the image of Jesus Christ. Just as Caesar guarantees the value of his coin, so the Father guarantees your value by the righteousness of God in Christ.

Acts 17:28 says, *"In Him we live, and move and have our being."* It's also true that in us He lives, and moves, and has His being.

God wanted them [the Jews] to know that the riches and glory of Christ are for you Gentiles, too. And this is the secret: Christ lives in you. This gives you assurance of sharing his glory. (Colossians 1:27 NLT)

Yes, all believers are in Christ and Christ is in them. If Jesus is full of grace and truth, so are we. What a wonderful message of reconciliation we have to share with everyone we meet.

So we are Christ's ambassadors; God is making his appeal through us. We speak for Christ when we plead, "Come back to God!" (2Corinthians 5:20)

I Can Forgive, But I'll Never Forget

Since we have been born again, are we more able to forgive others? How can we forgive and forget? The New Covenant encourages us to forgive others the same way God in Christ forgave us.

… be kind to each other, tenderhearted, forgiving one another, just as God through Christ has forgiven you. (Ephesians 4:32 NLT)

To forgive carries the meaning of separation. God's forgiveness toward us came about because He separated our sin from us and put it all on Christ. *For He* [God] *made Him who knew no sin* [Jesus] *to be sin for us, that we might become the righteousness of God in Him. (2Corinthians 5:21 NKJV)*

By faith, we no longer say, "You hurt me, so you're a bad person and I can't (or won't) forgive you." In Christ, we now say, "You hurt me, but you are still loved. I choose to separate the offense from you. I will no longer relate to you on that basis. I will continue to love you as Jesus does."

So… do we forgive and forget?

Let's look more closely at what God through Christ has done. God did not *forget* our sin; the Bible says He does not *remember* it anymore.

"*I, even I, am He who blots out your transgressions for My own sake; And I will not remember your sins. (Isaiah 43:25 NKJV)*

[God] *says, "I will never again remember their sins and lawless deeds." (Hebrews 10:17 NLT)*

To understand how this works, the English word, "remember," is an excellent illustration. "Re" means to do it again, such as rebuild or renew. "Member" means to be joined together, or connected.

So God is saying, "I will never again connect your sin to you." By separating the person from the offense, God provides complete forgiveness.

When we understand the forgiveness we have from God, we realize it is now in our new nature to forgive. We don't *forget* the wrongs done to us, but we intentionally choose to release a person from all obligation they may have toward us as a result of an offense. We no longer hold the offense against that person. Why? Because we *want* to release them, and because it is not our right to judge or condemn.

We do this not for them, but for our own sake. Again, we don't *forget* the offense, but we choose not to *remember* it. We can then walk in freedom from the bondage of unforgiveness, which easily turns into bitterness. The Bible calls bitterness a "root" that takes hold in our lives. The longer you let it grow, the more difficult it is to remove.

There was a time in my life when I held onto an offense far too long. It took root in my life and affected my joy and my attitude. My relationships suffered. One day I realized what I was doing and began to pray. I seldom have visions, but suddenly I saw something very clearly.

In the vision, a pair of hands reached into my mouth and began to pull out what looked like a vine. The hands kept pulling, hand over hand, for what seemed like a long time. Finally, it was out, and I sensed a powerful release in my spirit. I was able to let go of my unforgiveness and I began to restore damaged relationships. The root of bitterness was gone, and a great burden had been lifted!

As the well-known saying points out, to hold onto unforgiveness is like taking poison and then expecting the other person to die. Instead, it poisons our own lives and brings death to our peace, joy, and relationships. So, forgiveness truly is more for our benefit that for the benefit of the person who hurt us.

Jesus is always our example. While dying on the cross, He looked at those who murdered Him. His words, probably spoken between desperate gasps for breath, were these, *"Father, forgive them, for they don't know what they are doing."* (Luke 23:34 NLT) He didn't see them as murderers, but as people loved by the Father. He was able to separate their sin from them and see them as people in need of new life.

When we were born again, having put faith in Jesus, God gave us His Grace—the power of God in us to accomplish what we cannot accomplish on our own. We have the power of God through the Holy Spirit to forgive everyone, no matter how they have hurt us. It really is our choice, and the benefits are immediate and eternal.

The Freedom Of God's Grace

We hear Christians talk about "the grace message."
We also hear, "He (or she) teaches grace (or hyper-grace)."

But grace is not a message or a teaching, but a person—Jesus Christ. The entire gospel, the good news of Christ, is the freedom found in God's grace.

A Bible teacher who focuses on God's grace is focusing on Jesus Christ, the One who is *"full of grace and truth."* John also wrote, *"Grace and truth came through Jesus." (John 1:14, 17 NKJV)*

However, if we treat God's grace as a special revelation or a "camp" we lose the fullness of the gospel. Those who preach God's grace the way the apostle Paul did are not in the "grace camp;" they are simply proclaiming the grace-life of Christ.

God's grace and our faith work together for salvation.

God saved you by his grace when you believed. And you can't take credit for this; it is a gift from God. Salvation is not a reward for the good things we have done, so none of us can boast about it. (Ephesians 2:8-9 NLT)

Ephesians 2:8 in the NKJV says it this way, *"... by grace you have been saved through faith ..."* It's clear that salvation comes only by God's power as revealed through Jesus (grace) and through our absolute belief that this is true (faith). Grace is what God provides, faith is what we provide.

The New Covenant writers understood the riches of God's grace toward those who are born again. Those who are in Christ Jesus have:

- Freedom from the law or any performance-based system.
- Forgiveness of sin, past-present-future—once for all.
- No guilt, fear, or condemnation.
- 100% righteousness in Christ.
- The Holy Spirit within, empowering and teaching us.
- Eternal perfection; perfected forever.
- … and so much more, none of it deserved—all gifts from God!

But some will pervert this message and claim that the grace of God sets us free to live ungodly lives. This twisted interpretation also existed in the early church.

Dear friends, I had been eagerly planning to write to you about the salvation we all share. But now I find that I must write about something else, urging you to defend the faith that God has entrusted once for all time to his holy people.

I say this because some ungodly people have wormed their way into your churches, saying that God's marvelous grace allows us to live immoral lives. The condemnation of such people was recorded long ago, for they have denied our only Master and Lord, Jesus Christ. (Jude 1:3-4 NLT)

Clearly, any free-to-sin interpretation of grace is not approved by God. Scripture tells us the true effect that God's grace should have on our lifestyle. Far from promoting sin, grace teaches us to reject ungodliness and to live sober and righteous lives. Christ has redeemed us from the curse of the law, which is the strength of sin. So it is the law that energizes sin, and it is grace that produces Godly living. *(See Titus 2:11-14)*

…we are lying if we say we have fellowship with God but go on living in spiritual darkness [under the law]; *we are not practicing the truth* [which is grace]. *(1John 1:6 NLT)*

By his divine power, God has given us everything we need for living a godly life. We have received all of this by coming to know him, the one who called us to himself by means of his marvelous glory and excellence. (2 Peter 1:3 NLT)

So, while God's grace teaches us to live Godly lives, it's up to us to apply that truth through faith. The Holy Spirit leads us into all truth, encouraging and empowering us to live with purity and holiness. And our faith says, "I believe God is able to keep me pure, and His forgiveness is already there if I fail. Jesus' blood has washed away all my sin. I have been perfected forever. He has given me everything I need to live a Godly life."

The result is a Godly life lived in total freedom!

... if the Son sets you free, you are truly free. (John 8:36 NLT)

... Christ has truly set us free. Now make sure that you stay free, and don't get tied up again in slavery to the law. (Galatians 5:1 NLT)

The New Covenant is full of references to our being slaves to sin before Christ, and after we are saved we are dead to sin and free from its power. *(See Romans 6:14)* In the United States, we often hear, "Freedom isn't free." In the church, we can say the same because Jesus Christ freely gave Himself to purchase our freedom with His blood. Anytime we put ourselves back in slavery to a performance-based life we are, in effect, denying His words on the cross when He said, "It is finished!"

It's the grace of God, which is Jesus Himself, that makes all believers eternally free—free to be everything God wants us to be! All we have to do is believe it. Then we will live it!

Fruit Juice Saints–Just Squeeze

Lately, I've been studying the concept of "simplicity" in ministry. Sometimes the church gets caught up in theological complexity and academic perspectives. That approach may appeal to many, but to most it's not "simple." Look at Jesus' ministry. One of His main themes seems to be, "Be reconciled to God." And how did He do that?

... God anointed Jesus of Nazareth with the Holy Spirit and with power. Then Jesus went around doing good and healing all who were oppressed by the devil, for God was with him. (Acts 10:38 NLT)

He went around preaching, teaching, healing, loving. He wants us to do the same. So what does "went around" mean to us? It means to simply live our Christian lives in the world out there. And as we go, we let Him live His life through us, as us.

The Bible has many wonderful illustrations to show us how Christ does this. One has to do with fruit.

[Jesus said,] "Yes, I am the vine; you are the branches. Those who remain in me, and I in them, will produce much fruit. For apart from me you can do nothing.

Anyone who does not remain in me is thrown away like a useless branch and withers. Such branches are gathered into a pile to be burned.

But if you remain in me and my words remain in you, you may ask for anything you want, and it will be granted! When you produce much fruit, you are my true disciples. This brings great glory to my Father. (John 15:5-8 NLT)

How does one identify true or false prophets? You will know them by their fruit; by their lifestyle and what is produced by it. *(See Matthew 7:15-20)*

Okay, why "fruit" and not "vegetables" or "trees" or "flowers?" Jesus clearly is speaking of grapes when He speaks of fruit—the fruit of the vine. Everyone understood it. It was and is big business.

Have you ever bought grapes in a supermarket? They can look good on the outside, but sometimes they are sour, tasteless, or watery. You can't tell the quality of what's inside until you bite into them.

I like old movies. One is set in Italy at a huge vineyard. During the harvest, they put all the grapes in huge vats. The women took off their shoes and danced in the vats, crushing the grapes until the juice flowed out. The message? You can't make wine until you crush the grapes.

The Bible often speaks of the "juice" that comes out of our lives.

Now the works of the flesh are evident, which are: adultery, fornication, uncleanness, lewdness, idolatry, sorcery, hatred, contentions, jealousies, outbursts of wrath, selfish ambitions, dissensions, heresies, envy, murders, drunkenness, revelries, and the like…

But the fruit of the Spirit is love, joy, peace, longsuffering, kindness, goodness, faithfulness, gentleness, self-control. Against such there is no law. And those who are Christ's have crucified the flesh with its passions and desires. If we live in the Spirit, let us also walk in the Spirit. (Galatians 5:19-25 NKJV)

In the wine business, there are five basic characteristics that identify wine as good or not so good. These are sweetness, tannin, body, acidity, and fruitiness. Its goodness depends on the quality of the juice in the grapes.

In the above scripture, the fruit of the Spirit is *one* fruit, not nine. This one fruit has nine characteristics describing its quality— love, joy, peace, longsuffering, kindness, goodness, faithfulness, gentleness, self-control. The question for us is, "What comes out when we are squeezed; when the pressure is on?" The pressure can come from health, finances, travel, relationships, job stress, golf game, fishing, spouse, family, etc.

When we're squeezed does the fruit-juice of the Spirit come out, or do we respond in the flesh? *(See Galatians 5:19-25 again)* The squeezing reveals what's inside. It determines the taste of our lives to others, our maturity in Christ, and our attitude in the midst of the squeeze. The quality of our fruit is produced only through our release of the quality of Jesus' life in us.

The purpose of all New Covenant encouragements to do right and avoid wrong is to make sure we experience the abundant life Jesus promised, and not to earn points with God. They are to assure that the quality of our inner "juice" is excellent. God wants a rich and satisfying life for us because He loves us, and when we live that life in front of others it draws them to Him.

May you always be filled with the fruit of your salvation—the righteous character produced in your life by Jesus Christ—for this will bring much glory and praise to God. (Philippians 1:11 NLT)

When we go out and live our lives among people in the world, may our lives bring hope and joy to those around us. May we express the same love for others that God expresses toward us. When we're under pressure, or squeezed by the circumstances of our lives, may the sweet juice of the Spirit be released. This will reveal Jesus, full of grace and truth!

Do You Know Right From Wrong?

Here's an interesting question: Do born-again believers need to know right from wrong? Many will answer, "Well, of course! How else will we know what to do and what not to do? How else will we keep out of trouble?" That may sound right, but it's not *God's* answer.

It all started in the garden of Eden.

Then the LORD God planted a garden in Eden in the east, and there he placed the man he had made.

The LORD God made all sorts of trees grow up from the ground—trees that were beautiful and that produced delicious fruit. In the middle of the garden he placed the tree of life and the tree of the knowledge of good and evil. (Genesis 2:8-9 NLT)

These two trees represent two ways of living. First, the tree of life represents the life of God—Jesus Christ. When we are born again, He becomes our life.

For you died to this life, and your real life is hidden with Christ in God. And when Christ, who is your life, is revealed to the whole world, you will share in all his glory. (Colossians 3:3-4 NLT)

"I am the resurrection and the life. (John 11:25 NLT)

"I am the way, the truth, and the life." (John 14:6 NLT)

The question, "Do born-again believers need to know right from wrong?" is answered by God's instructions regarding the other tree in the middle of the garden:

And the LORD God commanded the man, saying, "Of every tree of the garden you may freely eat; but of the tree of the knowledge of good and evil you shall not eat, for in the day that you eat of it you shall surely die." (Genesis 2:16-17 NKJV)

This tree represents a system of rules and requirements. It's the tree of morality and immorality, of knowing right and wrong, of *self*-righteousness. God clearly said that His children don't need to know right from wrong, good from evil. He said, *"Of the tree of the knowledge of good and evil you shall not eat."*

He is saying, "You don't need to know right from wrong because you have Me." If we live out of our union with Christ we will always do what is right and never do what is wrong, all without memorizing a set of rules. When we ask, "Would it be right or wrong for me to do this?" we're asking the wrong question.

The right question is, "Will this behavior choice reveal Christ?" God wants us to let Jesus Christ live through us because He will always do the right thing. The issue is not about living an outwardly moral or immoral life because some unbelievers live more outwardly moral lives than some Christians. The life of Jesus is a miraculous life, not simply a moral life, and ours should be the same.

God warns against eating from that tree because it is the tree of religion, the tree of law-based life, the tree that leads to sin. That's why it causes death. It's all about trying and not about trusting. Yes, our behavior is important, but the issue is how our behavior is established—by trying or by trusting.

The serpent (Satan himself) lied to Eve about the effect of eating from the tree of the knowledge of good and evil by saying, *"God knows that your eyes will be opened as soon as you eat it, and you will be like God, knowing both good and evil."* (Genesis 3:5 NLT)

There are two lies here:

1. You are not like God.
2. There is something you can do to become like God.

The truth is:

1. She was already like God, created in His image.
2. There was nothing she could do to become more like God.

This is the same lie that religion teaches. "You want to be more like Christ? Then here is what you must do." Then we would hear a list of things to do and things to avoid in order to become more like Jesus. One thing religion fails to is mention the truth that once we are born again we are already like Jesus.

*By his divine power, God has given us **everything** we need for living a godly life. We have received **all** of this by coming to know him, the one who called us to himself by means of his marvelous glory and excellence. (2 Peter 1:3 NLT)*

Note the words, *everything* and *all*. Watchman Nee described it this way: "Oh, the folly of trying to enter a room that you're already in." That's the lie, that somehow we need more of God and can do something to get it. We believers already have *all* of Him.

This is the miracle of God's grace. It is a gift to be received, and not a goal to be achieved. After eating from the forbidden tree, Adam and Eve realized they were naked and thought, "Something is wrong. We are not presentable to God this way. We need a self-improvement program." This is the same thing religion says, "Examine yourself, and if you're not good enough, do what is necessary to make yourself presentable to God."

We still have the choice of trees from which to eat. Living by law or grace. Living by trying or trusting. Living by working or resting. Too many Christians have swallowed the bait and abandoned the tree of life for the tree of lies.

But doesn't the New Covenant speak of knowing right from wrong? Paul warns believers against a long-term diet of spiritual milk, meaning that they should avoid staying as babies. Then he says, *"… solid food belongs to those who are of full age, that is, those who by reason of use have their senses exercised to discern both good and evil. (Hebrews 5:14 NKJV)*

This ability to know good and evil doesn't come from a set of laws and rules. What we have as believers is a gift of the Holy Spirit called *discerning of spirits. (1Corinthians 12:10 NKJV)* Our understanding of right and wrong comes as we respond to the wisdom and direction of the Holy Spirit within us. This empowers us to clearly see what is of God and what is not.

So let's stop striving to figure out what is good and what is evil; let's stop trying hard to do good and avoid evil. Let's simply mature in our relationship with and knowledge of God, and trust Him to reveal Himself through us as we live our lives without pressure to perform in a certain way.

Here's a scripture you'll hear often from me: *For God is working in you, giving you the desire and the power to do what pleases him. (Philippians 2:13 NLT)* That's really good news!

Guilty As Charged

We have all done or said something we knew was wrong and then felt "guilty." In our politically correct culture guilt is out of control. We are condemned for things we say, do, or don't do. For many people, it seems like some measure of guilt never goes away.

The Old Testament religious system poured guilt on the Jews. God was seen as a stern, angry judge. The Old Testament Jew may have had his sins covered by the correct temple sacrifice, but by the end of the day, he was guilty again. Sin produced guilt and required sacrifice.

The Mosaic law of 613 points was like a chain. When working at a marina, I remember lifting a boat engine out of a hull with a hoist and chain. If one link should break, the engine would come crashing down, right through the hull, requiring major repair. For the Jew, one sin brought total destruction, so he would have to start over with new sacrifices to repair the damage.

For the person who keeps all of the laws except one is as guilty as a person who has broken all of God's laws. (James 2:10 NLT)

Sin-produced guilt was part of everyday life under the law.

The sacrifices under that system were repeated again and again, year after year, but they were never able to provide perfect cleansing for those who came to worship. If they could have provided perfect cleansing, the sacrifices would have stopped, for the worshipers would have been purified once for all time, and their feelings of guilt would have disappeared.

But instead, those sacrifices actually reminded them of their sins year after year. For it is not possible for the blood of bulls and goats to take away sins. (Hebrews 10:1-4 NLT)

This same practice of sacrifice exists today in just about every religious system—bloodless sacrifice known as "works" or getting busy doing things to appease or please God. The same guilt also exists. It's a feeling that we just didn't do enough and need to do more. We're guilty because of sins of commission and of omission, of failing to complete a task or mission in life.

There is a cure for guilt, for feeling like we have fallen short in some way and fearing that God is not pleased with us.

And so, dear brothers and sisters, we can boldly enter heaven's Most Holy Place because of the blood of Jesus. By his death, Jesus opened a new and life-giving way through the curtain into the Most Holy Place. And since we have a great High Priest who rules over God's house, let us go right into the presence of God with sincere hearts fully trusting him. For our guilty consciences have been sprinkled with Christ's blood to make us clean, and our bodies have been washed with pure water. **(**Hebrews 10:19-22 NLT)

The cross of Christ is the cure for sin and guilt. Sin and guilt are there, not here. To be guilty is to be held responsible for our mistakes, feeling like we failed and need to do something to fix it. It's like a burden that we can't unload.

But as believers, we don't have to carry it at all.

So now there is **no condemnation** *for those who belong to Christ Jesus. And because you belong to him, the power of the life-giving Spirit has freed you from the power of sin that leads to death.* (Romans 8:1-2 NLT)

No longer can any religious system condemn us; no longer can sin call us guilty. Through Jesus, we have been called righteous. Our righteousness comes from God, not from our performance.

I no longer count on my own righteousness through obeying the law; rather, I become righteous through faith in Christ. (Philippians 3:9 NLT) And *2Corinthians 5:21* affirms this fact by saying we *become* the righteousness of God.

Therefore, our righteousness is a state of *being* and not something that comes and goes. The same with our being *justified* and *forgiven* which are all states of *being*. This all means that we, His children, are also *not guilty* in God's eyes—ever.

But we say, "I know I'm all of those things, but I still feel guilty." If our feelings control our lives we will never be free. Feelings must bow to the truth about our relationship with God. Feeling guilty is a symptom of unbelief in the goodness of God.

You were dead because of your sins and because your sinful nature was not yet cut away. Then God made you alive with Christ, for he forgave all our sins. He canceled the record of the charges against us [declared us not guilty] *and took it away by nailing it to the cross. In this way, he disarmed the spiritual rulers and authorities. He shamed them publicly by his victory over them on the cross. (Colossians 2:13-15 NLT)*

Those who want to motivate Christians through guilt will say things like, "Jesus died for you, so you owe Him. What are you doing for Him? You better get busy. People are dying and going to hell because you aren't out there evangelizing."

Do you know how many verses of the Bible specifically call Christians guilty? None. Instead, we can express our confidence in the finished work of Christ on the cross and the power of the Holy Spirit within to lead us to maturity and transformation. Self-condemnation is not helpful; confidence in Christ is.

Let's say I do something that we would identify as 'sin.' I did do the unrighteous act, I missed the mark, yet God does not condemn me or pronounce me guilty. I have not damaged my relationship with God. He is not mad at me. I do not have to sacrifice or ask Him to forgive me to "restore fellowship" with Him. I am still righteous because it is something I am, not something I have.

What I *will* experience is the consequence of that action and the motivation to make things right as best I can. But under grace, God does not hold sin against me. *(See 2Corinthians 5:19)* If God isn't focusing on our sin, neither should we dwell on our weakness and failings. That only produces life-draining guilt. We now focus on our righteousness in Christ which gives us strength. That's where God is working.

We are being transformed, maturing in righteousness—not by *our* efforts, but by God Himself. We can rest in Him as He does the inward transformation. The result is simply to naturally do what pleases Him.

Are You Hungry and Thirsty?

In D.R. Silva's book, *It's All About Jesus*, he gives a helpful analysis of the popular concept that to be more spiritual we need to always be hungry and thirsty. Here are some insights from that chapter.

In *John 6* we read of Jesus' feeding thousands of people with five biscuits and two small fish. After everyone was satisfied, there were twelve baskets of leftovers, one for each disciple. A bona fide miracle!

The next day the crowd followed Him across the lake and when they found Him they asked, *"Rabbi, when did you get here?" Jesus replied, "I tell you the truth, you want to be with me because I fed you, not because you understood the miraculous signs. (See John 6:22-26 NLT)*

They got a good feeling and a full meal the last time they saw Him, so they came back for more. When we're experiencing an exciting, emotional time of worship we say or sing things like, "I'm desperate for you; I'm hungry for more of you; I'm thirsty for your Spirit." Are we really supposed to stay hungry and thirsty for God? Well, is God good? How good is He? Is He wealthy? Does He love His children? Is His love perfect and eternal?

If He is all these things, I don't think He'd leave His children desperate, hungry, or thirsty. Would He give them food and drink only if they came to Him and begged with tears, confessing how unworthy they are and how much they need more? I believe He would make sure His children were always supplied with an abundance of His attention, love, and power.

Our mindset and behavior will reveal what we believe about our relationship with God. Jesus talks to the people looking for a free lunch about the provision of God. Jesus said, *"The true bread of God is the one who comes down from heaven and gives life to the world." "Sir," they said, "Give us that bread every day." Jesus replied, "I am the bread of life. Whoever comes to me will **never** be hungry again. Whoever believes in me will **never** be thirsty. (John 6:33-35 NLT)*

If you look up the word "never" in the Greek you will find that it means "never." We need to learn to rest and trust in what God has provided. Away with songs and sermons that speak of us being in the desert place, or being desperate, hungry and thirsty, or wanting more of God. If we have a hard time receiving life and rest, it's because of our unbelief, and not because we are incomplete in Christ.

The devil encourages us to seek more of God so we will fail to see everything we have already been given. When we understand and apply what God has given us, we can exercise great power over our enemies—the world, the flesh, and the devil.

Paul warns us about this deception in *2Corinthians 11*. He says deceivers will teach about a different Jesus, a different kind of spirit, a different kind of Gospel. An extension of this deception is that somehow we believers run on battery power and need recharging when we run down, or that we leak the Holy Spirit and need to be refilled over and over. Any teaching that promotes a believer's spiritual incompleteness is a clear indication of religious thinking.

The truth is that we do not run on batteries. We are connected directly to the power source, God Himself. We are filled with the Holy Spirit at new birth and never leak any part of Him.

All praise to God, the Father of our Lord Jesus Christ, who has blessed us with every spiritual blessing in the heavenly realms because we are united with Christ. (Ephesians 1:3 NLT)

… in Christ lives all the fullness of God in a human body. So you also are complete through your union with Christ, who is the head over every ruler and authority. (Colossians 2:9-10 NLT)

… we have been given everything we need for life and godliness… (2Peter 1:3 NLT)

I have a deep desire for more knowledge and understanding of what I already have, not for what I'm told I don't have. This knowledge empowers me to lead a life of contentment and to be more effective for Christ in this world. There is no more to get, no matter how hard I try. The need for more of God is a myth that keeps us seeking and yearning, but never finding, never coming to the knowledge of the truth.

It does no good to ask God to come or come down, or to welcome Him into this place. He is already here and will never leave. We are *full* of Him, there is no room for anyone else—no darkness, no evil spirits.

God has put all things under the authority of Christ and has made him head over all things for the benefit of the church. And the church is his body; it is made full and complete by Christ, who fills all things everywhere with himself. (Ephesians 1:22-23 NLT)

The more we understand the fullness of His grace, the easier it is to sit down on the inside and enjoy His presence. Our greatest desire should be to sit at His feet and listen as Mary did. *(See Luke 10:38-42)* Jesus said about her, *"Mary has chosen that good part."* Then, when He assigns us a task, we move ahead in faith and power with great results!

Let's simply believe what Jesus said, *"Whoever comes to me will **never** be hungry again. Whoever believes in me will **never** be thirsty."*

The Hyper-Grace Loophole

Politicians, lawyers, stockbrokers—well, a great number of people—look for loopholes. Looking for a loophole is a selfish, prideful attempt to justify disobedience of laws or ethics with the goal of getting what we want without penalty. We may know what the *spirit* of the law is, but we want to bend the *letter* of the law to our own advantage.

The Bible tells us there are two ways to live our lives. All believers have a choice. *For those who live according to the flesh set their minds on the things of the flesh, but those who live according to the Spirit, the things of the Spirit. (Romans 8:5 NKJV)*

If we live according to the flesh, which is a desire to please ourselves outside of God, we search for loopholes that allow us to indulge ourselves and justify our actions. We might find justification in our culture, in our present circumstances, or even in the Bible.

One supposed Biblical loophole is in *Romans 7:14-25*. Paul says, "I want to do what is good, but I don't. I don't want to do what is wrong, but I do it anyway." (v.19) We might jump on that and say, "See? Paul messed up, so it's okay if I do, too!"

No, we need to read to the end of the passage where Paul says, *"Thank God! The answer is in Jesus Christ our Lord."* (v.25) This supposed loophole does not justify bad behavior because God has given us the ability to live according to the Spirit within us. It's a choice *we* make. The world, the flesh, and the devil can't force us to do anything.

So, let's say you hear the good news of grace the way the apostle Paul preached it. He taught that once we were saved we are *forgiven* as a state of being. This means that if we should sin we are already forgiven, with no penalty from God and no need to ask Him to forgive us. True, there are earthly consequences for our sin, but Christ already paid the price for all sin—past, present, and future—and the law is no longer our teacher. (I've dealt with these truths in other chapters, so I won't go into detail here.)

The religious mind fights this truth with great energy, denouncing it as an illegitimate "hyper-grace" teaching that encourages people to sin. While this might appear to be reasonable on the surface, we need to look more closely. We will find that the truth of hyper-grace teaching is indeed used as a loophole to sin, but only by Christians who live according to the flesh.

Believers who live according to the Spirit will not see grace in that light. They will see grace as the Bible teaches it. It is the power over sin, and it is the teacher who shows us how to live a Godly life. *(See Titus 2:11-14)*

More than once Paul exhorts the churches, "Should we sin so God will release more grace? God forbid!" And I say, "Should we stop preaching the fullness of grace so that believers who live according to the flesh won't be tempted to take advantage of it? God forbid!"

Using grace as a loophole to sin can't affect our right standing with God, but it will affect our ability to hear from the Holy Spirit. Sin will undermine our ministries, our human relationships, our attitudes, and our ability to love as Jesus loves. The believer who lives according to the flesh becomes selfish, hard-hearted, critical, and unloving.

The remedy is not to "stop it" or "just say no" because that never works as a genuine solution. The remedy is to encourage one another to believe that we do have power over sin, that we are free from the condemnation of the law, and that if we focus on the Holy Spirit we will experience the victory that has already been won for us. Instead of the fruit of the flesh, we will manifest the fruit of the Spirit. *(See Galatians 5:16-26)*

It's true that in the early stages of our Christian lives we will go through a childish phase, living in some ways according to the flesh. But the key is to "go through" it and come out with more maturity.

For those living according to the Spirit, the fullness of grace is a message of freedom and power over the world, the flesh, and the devil. The flesh says, "I *want* to sin, and I can justify it by grace." The Spirit says, "I *don't* want to sin and I can overcome temptation and condemnation through God's amazing grace."

God's law was given so that all people could see how sinful they were. But as people sinned more and more, God's wonderful grace became more abundant. So just as sin ruled over all people and brought them to death, now God's wonderful grace rules instead, giving us right standing with God and resulting in eternal life through Jesus Christ our Lord. (Romans 5:20-21 NLT)

In other English translations, different words are used to describe the extravagance of God's grace. Here are a few: superabounded; overabounded; abounded much more; multiplied even more; surpassed it and increased all the more.

The Greek word used to describe God's grace here is **hyper-eperisseusen**. Still another translation of this Greek word is "to extend beyond what already exceeds." The sense is that God's grace is not limited, that it always far exceeds the worst possible sinfulness. Paul, the great apostle, many times describes the grace of God as *hyper-grace*. He was the first hyper-grace preacher.

So let me be bold. If you are a believer using scripture or hyper-grace as a loophole to indulge in sin, you are walking according to the flesh. Jesus said, *"Repent of your sins and believe the Good News [the Gospel of grace]." (Mark 1:15 NLT)* It will truly change your life!

I Love The Church–But Which One?

A friend of mine gave me a book with the very long title, *Why We Love The Church; In Praise Of Institutions and Organized Religion.*

Perhaps I received the book because my friend was aware that my wife and I were no longer "members" of an institutional church but instead were focused on small-group meetings and Bible studies. Maybe I gave the impression that I was against denominational churches.

I read the whole book. I found it to be interesting, well written, honest and balanced. I understood perfectly the authors' message and had no quarrel with them. My 23 years as an institutional, denominational pastor helped me relate to their point of view.

When I laid the book down, a scripture came to mind. I encourage you to read it carefully. The apostle Paul wrote, *"I appeal to you, dear brothers and sisters, by the authority of our Lord Jesus Christ, to live in harmony with each other. Let there be no divisions in the church. Rather, be of one mind, united in thought and purpose.*

For some members of Chloe's household have told me about your quarrels, my dear brothers and sisters.

Some of you are saying, "I am a follower of Paul." Others are saying, "I follow Apollos," or "I follow Peter," or "I follow only Christ."

Has Christ been divided into factions? Was I, Paul, crucified for you? Were any of you baptized in the name of Paul? Of course not!" (1Corinthians 1:10-13 NLT)

Today we might write verse 12 like this: Some of you are saying, "I'm a member of the traditional institutional church," or, "I attend a house church," or, "I'm part of an organic fellowship," or, "My church meets on the golf course," or, "Three of us meet at Starbuck's for church."

Books have been written defending all these and other expressions of church, each lifting up the authors' particular method as being the best. Some go to extremes to attack other expressions as being inferior or even unscriptural.

Woe to us if we participate in this debate. It's just another divisive tactic of the enemy to make the church a mockery and ineffective. From time to time, I have been guilty of joining in. I have been wrong. Perhaps you, too, have expressed disdain for church meetings differing from your chosen style.

Your choice and my choice of Church expression should not create division. If we are in Christ and Christ is in us, then we can, if we will, live out this verse that bears repeating:

I appeal to you, dear brothers and sisters, by the authority of our Lord Jesus Christ, to live in harmony with each other. Let there be no divisions in the church. Rather, be of one mind, united in thought and purpose. (1Corinthians 1:10 NLT)

It took me the better part of six years to finally realize that this intense debate defending different kinds of church meetings is destructive to the Church itself. Remember that the Church is not the building, the denomination, or the style of worship. It is made up of born-again people, no matter how they express their faith.

There are only a few things that should cause us to flee from our chosen style of church fellowship. Some of these would be false teaching, ungodly manipulation, legalism, and a controlling spirit.

I'm aware that old thought patterns and biases die hard, slow deaths. Our desire should be to become more a part of the harmony and less of the division. Let's express the fullness of God's grace to all of our brothers and sisters in Christ, because there is only one church expressed in a myriad of ways.

*For there is **one** body and **one** Spirit, just as you have been called to **one** glorious hope for the future. There is **one** Lord, **one** faith, **one** baptism, **one** God and Father of all, who is over all, in all, and living through all. (Ephesians 4:4-6 NLT)*

Everything Is Possible With God

People who are faced with seemingly impossible situations often say, "Everything is possible with God." While that is true, the primary Biblical context of that statement is not just a general trust in the absolute power of God. The context is quite specific. It appears virtually the same in Matthew, Mark, and Luke, so it must be vital for us to understand. Malcolm Smith, a fine Bible teacher, has helped me to get a handle on this in his teaching, *Living the Impossible Life*. Let's explore.

*As Jesus was starting out on his way to Jerusalem, a man came running up to him, knelt down, and asked, "Good Teacher, what must I do to inherit **eternal life**?" (Mark 10:17 NLT)*

This man was very wealthy. He was proud of his ability to keep the Ten Commandments, but Jesus knew he was a slave to his wealth. When Jesus suggested that he sell everything, give the money to the poor, and then follow Him, the man walked away sadly. He couldn't do it.

*Jesus looked around and said to his disciples, "How hard it is for the rich to enter the **Kingdom of God**!"*

This amazed them. But Jesus said again, "Dear children, it is very hard to enter the Kingdom of God.

In fact, it is easier for a camel to go through the eye of a needle than for a rich person to enter the Kingdom of God!"

*The disciples were astounded. "Then who in the world can be **saved**?" they asked.*

*Jesus looked at them intently and said, "Humanly speaking, it is impossible. But not with God. **Everything is possible with God**." (Mark 10:23-27 NLT)*

In *verse 27* Jesus is answering a very specific question, *"Who in the world can be saved?"* The topic is *salvation*, which is impossible for anyone to achieve on his own. The camel illustration is humorous, intended to create a mental picture of an impossibility. The disciples were asking, "If the moral and the rich can't earn their way into the Kingdom of God, then who in the world can be saved?"

There are three things mentioned here that are impossible for any human to earn on his own. They are only possible with God: eternal life, the kingdom of God, and salvation.

What is Eternal Life? The average person's answer is usually vague: endless days, to live forever in heaven, etc.

However, *eternal* has little to do with time. It's more about the quality of life, not the quantity. It's an intensity of living, life as God lives it, experiencing His divine nature. We enter into eternity when we are born again.

[Jesus said,] *And this is eternal life, that they may know You, the only true God, and Jesus Christ whom You have sent. (John 17:3 NKJV)*

And this is what God has testified: He has given us eternal life, and this life is in his Son. Whoever has the Son has life; whoever does not have God's Son does not have life. (1 John 5:11-12 NLT)

We have the same life that Jesus has. In us is the fullness of the Godhead, the Holy Spirit, with all His gifts and power. It's much more than living forever. It's living His life right now, today. In *John 10:10* Jesus calls this the rich, satisfying, and abundant life of a new creation. We learn to live with Jesus expressing Himself through us, as us. It's a present moment thing.

What is the Kingdom of God? Typical answers might be, "It's out there somewhere, in the future. It's where God is king. It's God's rule in the hearts of men." Again, those are not very specific. Actually, God's Kingdom is His presence and His power at work today in the lives of His people.

[Jesus said,] "... if I cast out demons by the Spirit of God, surely the kingdom of God has come upon you." (Matthew 12:28 NKJV)

"Whatever city you enter, and they receive you, eat such things as are set before you. And heal the sick there, and say to them, 'The kingdom of God has come near to you.'"
(Luke 10:8-9 NKJV)

When God's will and purpose are being fulfilled, where His love is invading people's lives, where the people of God are ransacking the enemy's territory, there the kingdom of God has come. If the Holy Spirit is in us, then so is the kingdom of God. It is a present reality on earth today, not just in heaven someday.

What is salvation? A great many Christians answer, "I was saved from sin [past] and am going to heaven instead of hell when I die [future]." True, but what about right now? Do we just hang out until Jesus comes?

Salvation has very little to do with those things. The word means "wholeness, completeness, to be normal, all in harmony." We have been brought from confusion to orderliness, from all messed up to wholeness. The word "saved" was used other times when the sick were healed and the demon possessed were made free. They were made whole.

These three elements—eternal life, the kingdom of God, and salvation—together transform us into exactly what God wants us to be. God's life (eternal) comes into me; I become whole and complete (saved), and the Kingdom of God (His presence and power) shows up on earth.

We are fully equipped, and Jesus gives us His ministry:

God anointed Jesus of Nazareth with the Holy Spirit and with power, who went about doing good and healing all who were oppressed by the devil, for God was with Him. (Acts 10:38 NKJV)

If you are saved, you have this same anointing:

" ... *you have an anointing from the Holy One, and you know all things.*" *(1John 2:20 NKJV)*

We, too, can go about our daily lives doing good and healing, just like Jesus did. This is how God has always been! King David wrote, *"Be strong and courageous, and do the work. Don't be afraid or discouraged, for the Lord God, my God, is with you. He will not fail you or forsake you. (1 Chronicles 28:20 NLT)*

Law Living Is Not Fun Living

I was having breakfast with a group of Christian men when one of them shared about his life and his religious upbringing. For many years he and his parents were part of what he called a "legalistic" church. He said it wasn't much fun, and he kept looking over his shoulder to see if any church people were watching him. He always felt like God was ready to whack him with a big stick if he stepped out of established boundaries.

I think God wants our relationship with Him to be fun, joyful, free, exciting, and productive. *Sin is no longer your master, for you no longer live under the requirements of the law. Instead, you live under the freedom of God's grace. (Romans 6:14 NLT)*

When the Bible speaks of the law it refers to the hundreds of behavioral and activity requirements under the law of Moses. The church often says we are no longer under the law, and then produces its own set of rules. Here are some ways you can tell if you are living by law instead of grace.

1. You constantly battle self-condemnation.
The law is always condemning, critical, pointing out failures and faults. It always produces guilt by telling us when we are wrong, not doing enough, or that we will be blessed by certain behavior and cursed in some way by other behavior.

Remember that the law is called the ministry of death and the ministry of condemnation.

The old way, with laws etched in stone [the Ten Commandments], *led to death, though it began with such glory that the people of Israel could not bear to look at Moses' face. For his face shone with the glory of God, even though the brightness was already fading away.*

Shouldn't we expect far greater glory under the new way [grace], *now that the Holy Spirit is giving life?*

If the old way, [law] *which brings condemnation, was glorious, how much more glorious is the new way* [grace], *which makes us right with God! (2Corinthians 3:7-9 NLT)*

If we measure our spirituality by our behavior, we will feel self-condemned quite often. However, if I recognize God's love for me and truly understand who I am in Christ, then I have the desire and power to live a more Christ-like lifestyle. I am under no condemnation—not even my own. *(See Romans 8:1-3)*

2. You constantly struggle with sin.

The Bible clearly tells us that the strength of sin is law, which means that law will stir up sin in our lives.

When we were controlled by our old nature, sinful desires were at work within us, and the law aroused these evil desires that produced a harvest of sinful deeds, resulting in death. (Romans 7:5 NLT)

So, if we live our lives by a set of religious rules, we are actually fertilizing sin. The sin that we are desperately trying to get rid of is actually strengthened when we concentrate on getting rid of it. External requirements will never set us free. But God's grace teaches and empowers us to live holy lives through the Holy Spirit living within us. *(See Titus 2:11-12)*

When I first became a Christian it was a joy to read my Bible, because I really wanted to. I was then taught that a good Christian must read his Bible daily. It then became difficult to read consistently because it was a duty. We could say the same about prayer, church attendance, giving, serving, and many more "you-ought-to" commands.

3. You try to earn favor with God or maintain your relationship with God by doing good and avoiding evil.

But the people of Israel, who tried so hard to get right with God by keeping the law, never succeeded. Why not? Because they were trying to get right with God by keeping the law instead of by trusting in him. They stumbled over the great rock in their path.
(Romans 9:31-32 NLT)

Many Christians today are like those Jews. They read the old covenant law, then read the new covenant to find a new list of regulations, and mix it all together. They do their best to perform properly and in turn expect to earn favor with God. Of course, they fail at every step. No matter what we do, we cannot be more in favor with God, or more loved, or more appreciated.

When we put our trust in Jesus Christ, He gives us His righteousness. His way is not to work for it, but to receive it as a gift.

For the sin of this one man, Adam, caused death to rule over many. But even greater is God's wonderful grace and his gift of righteousness, for all who receive it will live in triumph over sin and death through this one man, Jesus Christ. (Romans 5:17 NLT)

The bottom line of the Gospel is that as a born-again child of God you are not *required* to conform to any external legal system. The only guide is the Holy Spirit who lives within each believer. And He gives us the *desire* to do what is right.

So, my dear brothers and sisters, this is the point: You died to the power of the law when you died with Christ. And now you are united with the one who was raised from the dead. As a result, we can produce a harvest of good deeds for God. (Romans 7:4 NLT)

When God Got His Hands Dirty

One of the great themes in scripture is God saying, "I am with you." Someone may ask, "Does that really mean 'all the time' or just when something disastrous happens? Is He involved daily in my finances, job, health, family, recreation, and all the other stuff I do?" And in the midst of trouble, we might be fatalistic and say, "Oh, well—that's life in this fallen world." The church often adds to our uncertainty about God's being involved in our earthly life by placing demands on us. Then we wonder, "Am I pleasing God, am I giving enough, am I serving enough, do I share the Gospel enough—how do I measure up?"

Many Christians see God as "up there" or "out there" somewhere, so His ways and thoughts seem to be far beyond us. We hear God speaking through the Bible, *"My thoughts are nothing like your thoughts,"* says the Lord. *"And my ways are far beyond anything you could imagine.*

"For just as the heavens are higher than the earth, so my ways are higher than your ways and my thoughts higher than your thoughts." (Isaiah 55:8-9 NLT)

Surely, we think, His concerns are for the *big* things, not the little challenges of our daily life. After all, He's in charge of the entire universe!

You may feel like an insignificant speck in the universe from God's perspective, but let's see what the Bible says about that. The Bible starts with these words in *Genesis,* "In the beginning, God created ..." God made all the stuff—dirt, food, animals, trees, mosquitoes—everything physical. Many times during His creation activities

He said, "It is good." Obviously, God is intimately involved in the physical creation, and He says that it's all good.

Let's take a closer look. When He made mankind, he got His hands dirty—if we can think of God having hands—by digging in the dirt.

*And the LORD God **formed** man of the dust of the ground, and breathed into his nostrils the **breath of life**, and man became a living being. (Genesis 2:7 NKJV)*

Not only did he dig in the dirt and shape the first human with His hands, but He also put His divine breath into that physical human body. That's being intimately involved. Just a comment—Adam probably didn't have a belly button.

Then He created Eve from a rib taken out of Adam. The Great Physician performed major surgery and then, by hand, formed a woman. She didn't have a belly button, either.

After Adam and Eve sinned, God got His hands bloody when He killed an animal and made coverings for them.

And the LORD God made clothing from animal skins for Adam and his wife. (Genesis 3:21 NLT)

Throughout the Old Testament, we see God involved in the daily lives of His people. God was so connected with His physical creation that He became a part of it in Jesus, God of very God born fully human. God Himself joined the physical realm—in person.

During His lifetime on earth, Jesus played with other children, the girls probably flirted with Him, He went to school and took tests, worked in His father's carpenter shop building with stone and wood with His bare hands. He got His hands dirty. He shopped in the market, went to weddings, laughed, danced. He went to funerals and wept. He got involved in people's lives. He lived under Roman occupation. He paid taxes to Caesar and to the temple. He was involved in religious worship and participated in all the feasts of the Lord.

After His baptism, the God-man, Jesus, continued to get His hands dirty in the physical realm. He touched the leper, the prostitute, the sick, the blind and the dead—the outcasts of society. Many of them were considered unclean and anyone who touched them would be considered defiled, or dirty. Under Jewish law, if the clean touched the unclean, the clean became dirty and needed to wash. When Jesus (the clean one) touched the unclean, the unclean became clean and Jesus remained clean! (Did you follow that okay?)

After His resurrection, He continued to walk in the physical realm. He ate fish, people touched Him and heard Him. He was there in the same physical form as He now is in heaven. Right now, Jesus is in heaven in a physical, glorified human body.

And today God would say to us, "I am still involved with you in everything you do. I get my hands dirty with you. I am in you and living My life through you. Your hands are My hands." He's not only God up there, He is also God down here, right now. His involvement in the here and now should eliminate our concerns. He is God of heaven and earth, deeply involved in both realms. He is willing to dig into the earthly realm and get His hands dirty as he works alongside us every day.

And not only is God with us at all times and in all things, He is also **for** us. He is on our side. He is rooting for us in the game of life.

*What then shall we say to these things? If **God is for us**, who can be against us? He who did not spare His own Son, but delivered Him up for us all, how shall He not with Him also freely give us all things? (Romans 8:31-32 NKJV)*

Here's something you can repeat in challenging moments, "God is *with* me and God is *for* me! What can this world do to me?" He is never angry at the dumb things we say and do. He always with us and is always on our side, working to transform us and help us. Count on it!

Let There Be Light!

While reading the story of creation in *Genesis*, I found something that puzzled me.

Day One: *In the beginning, God created the heavens and the earth. The earth was formless and empty, and darkness covered the deep waters. And the Spirit of God was hovering over the surface of the waters. (Genesis 1:1-2 NLT)*

The earth was in absolute darkness, apparently in confusion and disorder. Nothing physical existed on the earth except water with the Spirit of God hovering over it like a hen broods over her eggs, waiting for something to hatch.

Then God said, "Let there be light," and there was light. (Genesis 1:3 NLT)

Day Two: The Earth received an atmosphere.

Day Three: Dry ground appeared and God created all kinds of vegetation.

Day Four: This is the day that puzzled me. On day four God created the sun and the moon to separate the day from the night and to give light. Wait a minute! There was light on day one!

So where did the day-one light come from? In *Genesis 1:1* we read that God created the heavens and the earth. Then, in the next verse, for whatever reason, the earth was in total darkness with no life and no order. We call it *chaos*. There are many theories about this, but they're not pertinent to this discussion.

In the midst of this chaos, God entered into His physical creation. When God enters, so does light, because God is light *(See 1John 1:5)*. In Him, there is no shadow, no darkness. So when He said, "Let there be light" He was really saying, "Let there be ME!"

… he lives in light so brilliant that no human can approach him. (1 Timothy 6:16 NLT)

And in *James 1:17* we are told that He is the Father of lights.

We also know that Jesus was given the task of creation:

… through him [Jesus] God created everything in the heavenly realms and on earth.

… Everything was created through him [Jesus] and for him. (Colossians 1:15-16 NLT)

So, the day-one light of creation came from the presence of God and Jesus Christ, the eternal sources of divine light. The Bible tells us that heaven's New Jerusalem has no need for the sun or moon because the glory of God and the lamb (Jesus) are its light. *(See Revelation 21:23)*

When God, in the person of Jesus, lived on earth, He was the source of divine light and life for all humanity.

In Him [Jesus] was life, and the life was the light of men. (John 1:4 NKJV)

The Word [Jesus] gave life to everything that was created, and his life brought light to everyone. (John 1:4 NLT)

Notice the connection between His light and His life:

Jesus spoke to the people once more and said, "I am the light of the world. If you follow me, you won't have to walk in darkness, because you will have the light that leads to life." (John 8:12 NLT)

In the natural realm, what are some things light does?

- Light dispels darkness.
- Light reveals hidden things (such as cockroaches).
- Light attracts attention, such as police lights or a strobe light on an airplane.

- Light warms like the Florida sun.
- Light brings life to plants and all living things.
- Light produces color. White light passed through a prism reveals a rainbow of color.

The divine light of Jesus does all of this and more in the spiritual realm. In addition, Jesus said we, His followers, are the light of the world.

"You are the light of the world … Let your light so shine before men, that they may see your good works and glorify your Father in heaven." (Matthew 5:14, 16 NKJV)

Live clean, innocent lives as children of God, shining like bright lights in a world full of crooked and perverse people. (Philippians 2:15 NLT)

Yes, we are to be the source of divine light for this world.

- To expose deception (darkness) through spiritual truth (light).
- To attract attention to Jesus.
- To warm people's hearts and lives.
- To bring new life through His Word and our testimony.
- To produce colorful, interesting, attractive lives.

Oswald Chambers wrote that the light of Christ is a "present moment" thing. It must be available immediately when needed or it is no good at all. Our Christian lives are designed to shine at all times.

Matthew 5:15 tells us not to hide our light under a basket, but to let it give light to everyone. Let's not hide His light under a basket of sin, selfishness, pride, arrogance, or any other ungodly practice.

For you are all children of the light and of the day; we don't belong to darkness and night. (1 Thessalonians 5:5 NLT)

For once you were full of darkness, but now you have light from the Lord. So live as people of light! (Ephesians 5:8 NLT)

As believers, we are filled with the light and life of Jesus in the person of the Holy Spirit. As such, our attitude, language, compassion, and behavior are to reflect the very nature of Christ. This is not something we work up and try hard to produce. This is something that simply *is*. It all comes out of us naturally, because we are Spirit-filled people.

It's interesting to note that there is no such thing as darkness. There is only the absence of light. The smallest lit candle will invade a dark room with its light. And when a believer enters a crowded room, His light will light up the darkness surrounding those who don't know Him. In fact, God spiritually announces our arrival by saying, "Let there be light—My light that brings My life." We can make a big difference. This little light of mine; let it shine!

Who Wears Linen Underwear?

I have some linen shirts. They look great when they come back from the cleaners. However, after wearing them just once they look like I wore them to bed and had a fitful night's sleep. They get wrinkled beyond home ironing. As for wearing linen underwear, I would not be a fan—not because they wrinkle easily (who cares about wrinkled underwear, anyway?) but because the fabric seems to be stiff and uncomfortable.

So I was curious as to why the Old Testament priests were required to wear linen undergarments, and what that might mean to a New Testament believer in Christ. What I found out is interesting, even though underwear is not usually a topic for polite conversation. Here is God's instruction about how to dress as a temple priest:

"When Aaron enters the sanctuary area, he must follow these instructions fully. ... He must put on his linen tunic and the linen undergarments worn next to his body. He must tie the linen sash around his waist and put the linen turban on his head. These are sacred garments, so he must bathe himself in water before he puts them on. (Leviticus 16:3-4 NLT)

"When they [the priests] enter the gateway to the inner courtyard, they must wear only linen clothing. They must wear no wool *while on duty in the inner courtyard or in the Temple itself. They must wear linen turbans and linen undergarments. They must not wear anything that would cause them to perspire. (Ezekiel 44:17-18 NLT)*

Linen was symbolic of righteousness. It was made from flax, a natural organic material. Linen breathes more than cotton and minimizes sweating in hot conditions—as it would be around the burning sacrifices on the altar.

This is a shadow of the royal priesthood of all those who are born again. *(See 1Peter 2:5, 9)* It looks forward to the believer being spiritually dressed in the priestly garments of the New Covenant. When I put on the Lord Jesus Christ *(See Galatians 3:27)* I am clothed in His righteousness, purity, and holiness.

In addition, my position in Him is one of rest. The linen garment reduces perspiration, or sweat. *(See Ezekiel 44:18)* In Christ, there's no need to sweat and exert our own efforts to earn righteousness. We can rest on Christ's performance, not ours, and simply receive righteousness as a gift.

For all who have entered into God's rest have rested from their labors, just as God did after creating the world. (Hebrews 4:10 NLT)

The work we do now is in obedience to the Holy Spirit, and He gives us the energy and power to complete it without sweating or striving in our own strength.

The Old Testament priests had to bathe before putting on their linen garments. Those who are born again are bathed in the blood of Christ, which cleanses from all sin. He then provides the priestly garments of righteousness. Isaiah proclaimed, *"I am overwhelmed with joy in the Lord my God! For he has dressed me with the clothing of salvation and draped me in a robe of righteousness. I am like a bridegroom dressed for his wedding or a bride with her jewels." (Isaiah 61:10 NLT)*

Remember when Jesus told the parable of the King's wedding feast? *(See Matthew 22:11-13)* The person who showed up without the proper wedding garment was thrown into outer darkness. People who try to sneak into the presence of Christ without their linen garments (a relationship with Him) will be thrown out.

At the end of time, there will be a glorious wedding feast in heaven when the bride (the church) is eternally united with the groom (Jesus Christ).

Let us be glad and rejoice and give Him glory, for the marriage of the Lamb has come, and His wife has made herself ready." And to her it was granted to be arrayed in fine linen, clean and bright, for the fine linen is the righteous acts of the saints. (Revelation 19:7-8 NKJV)

Unlike today's fashion of flaunting your underwear, true holiness begins internally as a gift from God—it's not physically visible. For example, when you first meet a person you have no idea what kind of spiritual underwear he's wearing.

However, the description of the priestly linen garments does not end with the underwear. It has to be put on first, of course, but then other linen garments are put on over the underwear. There are the ephod, robe, sash, turban, etc.

In other words, it's important that the nature of Christ in us (the part that is hidden) is revealed to others. Our behavior, attitudes, and good works should be an accurate representation of the nature of God. The righteousness of Christ within, in the person of the Holy Spirit (the underwear), transforms our behavior (the outerwear) from glory to glory into the image of Christ. *(See 2Corinthians 3:18)*

As my mom used to say, "Be sure to put on clean underwear in case you get into an accident." Thank God our spiritual underwear is always clean. And if we should accidentally sin, it remains clean because of our righteousness in Him!

The Love Of Grace

Just as a car needs fuel to run, so our lives need fuel. Things we eat or drink are the fuel that produces the energy we need for our physical lives, and things we see, hear, think and feel are the fuel that produces the energy we need for our soul and spirit. God's unconditional love for us is the fuel that produces His grace, which is the energy of the believer's entire life.

The law of Moses is not fuel for grace. Perhaps you have heard this passage: *You shall love the Lord your God with all your heart, with all your soul, and with all your strength. (Deuteronomy 6:5 NKJV)* Do you realize that this is *not* one of the Ten Commandments? It is part of what the Jews call the *Shema Yisrael* found in *Deuteronomy 6:4-9*. Jesus quoted this same passage in *Matthew 22* where He calls it the greatest commandment in the law. It is rightly based on the first commandment, that we should worship no other gods.

It is, however, still a commandment, one that no one has ever fully obeyed except Jesus Christ. But God, through the New Covenant of grace, says, "I love you this much!" And He spread His arms and died. He loved us long before we even thought of loving Him.

John the apostle realized God's love for him. He called himself "the disciple whom Jesus loved." Five times he referred to himself that way. He wasn't being arrogant but was simply practicing and celebrating Jesus' love for him. In one of his letters he writes, *"… we have known and believed the love that God has for us. (1 John 4:16 NKJV)*

John *knew* and *believed* that God loved him.

The law says good things happen to those who love God and prove it by their behavior and performance. Grace says good things happen to those who know and believe God loves them without any conditions. They become stable, secure, confident, without fear, and free from bondage. Out of that knowledge and belief springs a love for God that we could never experience apart from His love for us.

*And may you have the power to **understand**, as all God's people should, how wide, how long, how high, and how deep his love is.*

*May you **experience** the love of Christ, though it is too great to understand fully. Then you will be made complete with all the fullness of life and power that comes from God.*

Now all glory to God, who is able, through his mighty power at work within us, to accomplish infinitely more than we might ask or think… (Ephesians 3:18-20 NLT)

Note what happens when we *understand* and *experience* the love Christ has for us. We receive the fullness of life and power, and accomplishments beyond anything we can imagine!

At the Last Supper meal, both law and grace were represented. Peter represented the law, boasting about his love for Jesus. He said things like, "I'm ready to go to prison or die for you," and, "If all others leave you I never will!" John represented grace, boasting on Jesus' love for him. At the meal, John was actually leaning on Him. Peter asked John to find out from Jesus who would betray Him. Peter didn't feel close enough to Jesus to ask on his own but saw in John the intimacy he didn't believe he had.

Law says "I love Jesus." Grace says, "Jesus loves me." Take note of this verse:

*We love Him because He **first** loved us. (1 John 4:19 NKJV)*

The word, *Him*, is not in the original text, so it properly reads, *"We love because He first loved us."* We have the power to love because God loved us first.

God loves *all* His children, even the angry, bitter, rebellious ones. His love for us is what matters most, not our love for Him. His love for us is what makes us free indeed.

Religion tells us to work hard at loving God because the Bible says we *must*. But *Matthew 11:28-30* quotes Jesus' promise to give us rest from these kinds of demands. He said, "Come to Me for rest." *Hebrews 4* also speaks of rest:

There remains, therefore, a rest for the people of God. For he who has entered His rest has himself also ceased from his works as God did from His. (Hebrews 4:9-10 NKJV)

Rest is not inactivity or laziness, but soul rest. The striving, guilt, fear, and condemnation has ended in Christ. He doesn't *require* performance in order to produce our righteousness or to earn His acceptance.

We might tell someone, "God loves you." They may reply, "Sure, I know, God loves everybody." While that's true, that's not God's focus. God's focus is intensely personal. If we see ourselves as part of a group, then we lose the intimate nature of His love for each of us. John, the disciple whom Jesus loved, didn't feel like one of the crowd. He felt like *the one*. This love-fueled grace produces faith that empowers us to overcome fear, rejection, anger, frustration, and a host of other paralyzing attitudes and behaviors.

Can anything ever separate us from Christ's love? (See Romans 8:35-39 NLT) Thank God the answer is, of course, "No!" And the more we realize this truth, the more we will, in turn, love Him in a way that makes Jesus visible and attractive to those around us.

Lunchtime Seeds–A Short Drama

Here's a short drama I wrote several years back for a church youth event. Let's exercise our imaginations and visit a high-school school cafeteria where we meet two girls, Ginger and Amanda. Ginger is a party girl, popular, and loves to have a good time. Amanda is a Christian and wants to live according to Biblical principles. She is a bit shy and has been curious about what Ginger does at her parties. As the drama begins they are opening the lunches they brought from home.

Ginger: *(Looks at her sandwich)* Gross! Egg salad with olives in it! Sometimes I think my Mom is out to poison me! *(Looks at Amanda's lunch and makes a face)* What's that?!

Amanda: Liverwurst and pickles, onions, lettuce, and mayo.

Ginger: *(Not believing her ears)* You gonna *eat* it?!

Amanda: *(Smiling)* Well, yeah. I ordered it that way.

Ginger: I'll order a stomach pump. *(Looks at her own sandwich)* This looks pretty good, after all. *(She takes a bite, begins chewing, and suddenly stops. Her eyes open wide, looking shocked, and she points out over the audience)*

Amanda: Are you all right?

Ginger: It's him! It's really him! Oh my gosh! I can't stand it!

Amanda: *(Looks to where she's pointing)* Who? Who? Who?

Ginger: You sound like an owl. *(Points again)* Jimmy Martinez. Right there, by the candy machine. He is super hot! *(Sighs and looks at Amanda)* But I haven't got a chance.

Amanda: Why?

Ginger: Because he likes *you*, that's why!

Amanda: *(Confused)* Huh? Me? But I've never met him.

Ginger: Oh, he likes you, all right. My boyfriend, Kevin, is good friends with him. *(Confidentially)* And he told me that Jimmy wants to ask you out but he's afraid you won't go. *(A sudden idea)* Hey— I can set it up! We'll all go out together; me and Kevin and you and Jimmy.

Amanda: Yeah, he is kind of cute. But where would we go? *(Looks concerned)* On second thought, I've heard some pretty wild things about him. Maybe it wouldn't be a good idea, after all.

Ginger: Wild? He just knows how to have a good time. *(Confidentially)* I hear his car has a really comfortable back seat. *(She giggles)*

Amanda: *(Embarrassed)* Ah, well— I don't really think we'd get along.

Ginger: *(Sarcastic)* I suppose you want to take him to church. *(Laughs)* I'll bet he can't even *spell* church! *(A little upset)* You know, Amanda, sometimes you get on my nerves. You think you're better than us because you go to church a lot?

Amanda: *(Defensive, unsure)* No, not really. I mean— well— it's not going to church, exactly—

Ginger: *(More upset)* Well, what is it, then? You never come to our parties, you never fool around with guys, you never seem to have a good time. *(Intense, in her face)* You're boring, Amanda, boring!

Amanda: *(Meek, defensive)* I'm sorry you feel that way. Maybe I should just go away and hide, then.

Ginger: *(Tries to persuade her)* Look— I like you. I don't know why, but I do. I just want you to have some fun. A little beer, a little car ride out in the country, a little— well, you know. *(Leans in closely)* Amanda, it *feels good* to have fun!

Amanda: *(Softening)* Well, maybe I could go to a party someday, but not with someone like Jimmy. He's cute, but—

Ginger: I suppose you want to go out with a guy like Caleb Bullard. *(Sarcastic)* He's a real gem—goes to church as much as you do.

Amanda: *(Smiling, more confident)* I've been out with Caleb, and we had a great time. We played tennis and then went swimming. We have a lot in common.

Ginger: Sounds too healthy to me. You need more than tennis and swimming in common to have a good time.

Amanda: We do have more in common. *(Unsure about what she's going to say, and says it very quietly)* We have Jesus in common.

Ginger: *(Leans in closer)* Say what?

Amanda: *(More boldly)* We have Jesus in common.

Ginger: *(Stands up suddenly)* What? Who? Jesus? The religious Jesus? The one in the Bible?

Amanda: *(Still more boldly, smiling)* That's the one— Jesus Christ!

Ginger: *(Sits down and leans in closely)* Not so loud! Are you out of your mind? *(Shakes her head and looks around to see who's looking)* And I'm sitting at the same table! What if somebody thinks I have the same problem? I'm outta here. *(Stands up to go)*

Amanda: *(To stop her)* I've been praying for you.

Ginger: *(Somewhat upset)* What? Praying? You stop that! Stop that right now! I don't need anyone praying for me— especially some Jesus weirdo. *(Amanda looks hurt, and Ginger sits down and softens)* Hey, I'm sorry. I didn't really mean that, but—well, you took me by surprise. Nobody I know talks about Jesus except to curse.

Amanda: *(After a moment of silence)* He loves you, you know.
Ginger: *(Uncomfortable)* Who? Jimmy or your Jesus? *(Laughs uneasily)*
Amanda: *(Now she's comfortable)* Jesus gives me peace, Ginger. Love, happiness, and a real help when I need it.
Ginger: *(Not sure, bluffing)* Look—I can handle my own problems. Sure don't need no invisible friend. *(Leans in so no one can hear)* But sometimes my *visible* friends ain't too sweet. *(Pause—then seriously and confidentially)* I'm not always happy, you know.
Amanda: I know.
(The school bell rings)
Ginger: Well, I guess we gotta go to class. *(Stands up reluctantly)*
Amanda: *(Standing)* I'd like to talk some more, sometime.
Ginger: *(Sincerely)* Yeah, I suppose we could do that. Maybe tomorrow at lunch. See ya. *(She walks off slowly, thinking, looks back and smiles.)*
(Amana watches her walk away, smiling, waves when she turns back)

Curtain

A person like Ginger, who is not a follower of Jesus, will not find condemnation from Him no matter what she's done. Instead, she will find mercy and grace. She will find an invitation to forgiveness, an intimate relationship with Him, and power to overcome every temptation.

If you are a believer, what kinds of seeds are you planting in the lives of those who don't know Jesus? Are you planting seeds of condemnation, or when they look for help will you plant seeds of mercy and grace while maintaining your own purity?

Jesus says to all believers, *"Go and announce to [the unsaved] that the Kingdom of Heaven is near. Heal the sick, raise the dead, cure those with leprosy, and cast out demons. Give as freely as you have received!" (Matthew 10:7-8 NLT)*

Jesus was always willing to reach out and touch anyone, so our willingness to do the same should be no less. Who knows? One day an unbeliever may look you in the eye and say, "I believe it's true. I'm ready to give up my life for His." That would be awesome!

Must I Forgive To Be Forgiven?

Here's a challenging statement for many believers who grew up in the traditional, institutional church environment. "Not everything Jesus said is binding on those who are born again—those who are saved by grace through faith in Christ." This understanding is vital for believers when they have the opportunity to work through problems of their own or with family or friends.

Christian counseling can be effective in helping people cope with life issues and difficulties. The key is to focus on New Covenant principles and to recognize the dramatic changes that took place between the Old Testament and the New Covenant. If we're not careful, we might give advice and counsel that doesn't recognize the freedom of God's grace for the believer.

One of the most pervasive issues believers face is misunderstanding forgiveness. Because of this, I've covered some of this material in other chapters. But let's walk through some background to come up with a Biblical answer to the question, "Must I forgive to be forgiven?"

The Old Testament, through the law, rightly viewed people as sinners—people whose lives were dominated by sin. In that lost condition, they could not have intimacy with God.

It's your sins that have cut you off from God. Because of your sins, he has turned away and will not listen anymore. (Isaiah 59:2 NLT)

The Old Testament sacrifices provided a covering for *past* sins through the blood of animal sacrifices, but *new* sins had to be covered by the blood of more sacrifices. This continuing cycle never touched man's sin nature. We can't do anything about it on our own, and we are slaves to sinful behavior. The old system of law reveals our utter inability to be Godly without God.

What's needed is total forgiveness, the removal of our sin nature and elimination of the penalty for all our sinful actions—past, present, and future. Jesus Christ is the remedy. Paul wrote, *"You were dead because of your sins and because your sinful nature was not yet cut away. Then God made you alive with Christ, for he forgave all our sins. He canceled the record of the charges against us and took it away by nailing it to the cross." (Colossians 2:13-14 NLT)*

John the baptizer pointed at Jesus and said, *"Look—the Lamb of God who takes away the sin of the world." (John 1:29)* And *1John 1:9* promises that once we are forgiven we are cleansed from *all* unrighteousness. It's a once-for-all-time cleansing.

At the cross, Jesus took on Himself the sin nature of the entire world and all the sins that resulted from it. His death provided for complete forgiveness from God, spiritual perfection for believers, and an intimate relationship with God. Once we believe this is true, and put our faith in the living Jesus, we are born again and receive all these benefits.

The law in the Old Testament said, and traditional Christianity today often says, "If you don't forgive others, God will not forgive you." Jesus spoke this principle from the law in *Matthew 6:14-15* and *Mark 11:25-26*. As He did many times, He was using the law for its intended purpose—to reveal that no one can make himself righteous through his own effort. So Jesus was not saying something that is binding on Christians today, but was leading people from self-righteousness to God righteousness.

Think about it. If you try to obey this strict forgiveness demand, you will always be frustrated, fearful, and uncertain about God's forgiveness. You'll think, "Maybe I'm still holding a grudge, maybe I haven't really forgiven everybody who ever hurt me, maybe God is withholding His forgiveness."

His disciples were amazed and disheartened when Jesus taught that they should forgive the same offense 70 times seven, or 490, times. *(See Matthew 18:21-22)* I'm sure they thought, "That's impossible! Nobody can do that!" and they were right.

Grace says, "You forgive others because God *has forgiven* you." Do you see the difference? God's forgiveness comes first—then I can forgive others. Paul wrote, *"… be kind to each other, tenderhearted, forgiving one another, just as God through Christ has forgiven you."* (Ephesians 4:32 NLT)

Forgiveness is the perfect demonstration of God's love for us. When we were born again, and before we had a chance to forgive anyone else, God totally forgave all our sins—past, present, future—regardless of our performance in forgiving others. Christ's sacrifice made it unnecessary to "earn" God's forgiveness by forgiving others. We became forgiven people as a state of *being*, not of becoming. Now, by the power of God's grace, we have the ability to totally forgive those who have hurt us.

Look again at that verse we started with from Isaiah, where God turned away from His people because of their sin. The new covenant of God's grace began at the cross of Christ. Jesus became sin for us, and God turned away from Him so He would **never** have to turn away from us. And that's good news!

Who's Guarding Your Gates?

The gates of ancient cities were extremely busy places. Just inside the gates, many civic activities took place—legal, business, news, buying and selling, reading the Torah, and, of course, plenty of gossip.

King David wrote, *"I am the favorite topic of town gossip, and all the drunks sing about me." (Psalm 69:12 NLT)*

The gate was the only way in and out of a walled city. Huge doors or metal gates were in place to protect the inhabitants. The gate opening was often just wide enough for single chariots and carts to pass through. Prophets proclaimed at the gate. Criminals were punished outside the gate. Travelers slept just inside the gate if they had no place to go. Towers were built at the gate to see who was coming from a distance. There might be hidden places inside the gate, above and to the sides, where defenders could throw down boiling liquids and rocks on attackers.

… the LORD of hosts will be for a crown of glory and a diadem of beauty to the remnant of His people, for a spirit of justice to him who sits in judgment, and for strength to those who **turn back the battle at the gate**. *(Isaiah 28:5-6 NKJV)*

The place to turn back the enemy is at the gate. Judges interviewed strangers coming in, and would not allow the dishonest or corrupt to enter. Once inside, past the authority of the elders, a visitor had permission to be there. If that visitor happened to be dangerous, it was very difficult to remove him.

Today our cities are open. There are no walls, no gates, and no judges to interview visitors. The city hall is the place of justice, church buildings are where scripture is read, and stores are where goods are sold. There's virtually no control over who comes and goes.

We can apply the city-gate principle to ourselves today. We have control over the gates of our homes, our families, and our lives. Everything that comes into our homes should be evaluated. Without being paranoid about it, we need to take a Godly look at guests, books, magazines, music, videos, television programs, computers, games, etc. We ask ourselves, "If I allow this into my home, will this be good for our household or not? Is this something God would endorse?" Remember, once it's inside it's hard to remove.

God also tells us to guard the gates of our personal lives. We have many gates that lead into our minds and our bodies. Our eyes, ears, hands, mouths, and noses are all gates to our inner selves. Things that enter through those gates can enrich us or corrupt us. Our five "senses" receive and process what they encounter, and they do shape our lives.

The Word of God in our minds and hearts will help us evaluate everything that enters. We can protect ourselves and our families by setting a Godly standard, living by it, and encouraging the family to live by it. Jesus said, *"Enter by the narrow gate; for wide is the gate and broad is the way that leads to destruction, and there are many who go in by it. Because narrow is the gate and difficult is the way which leads to life, and there are few who find it. (Matthew 7:13-14 NKJV)*

I believe this verse has nothing to do with our eternal destination, hell or heaven, but much to do with the quality of our lives while on earth.

The word used here is *destruction*, not hell. If it meant hell, it would clearly say it.

The word used here is *life*, not heaven. If it meant heaven, it would clearly say it.

Jesus is telling us that we have a choice in our earthly lives to either embrace the abundant life He came to provide (the narrow, difficult gate), or to live only for ourselves and experience a more destructive life (the wide, easy gate).

Jesus affirmed this when He said, *"I tell you the truth, I am the gate for the sheep. All who came before me were thieves and robbers. … Yes, I am the gate. Those who come in through me will be saved. They will come and go freely and will find good pastures. The thief's purpose is to steal and kill and **destroy**. My purpose is to give them a rich and satisfying **life**. (John 10:7-10 NLT)*

We don't have to let the enemy fulfill his destructive purpose. However, it's not a good idea to make our homes legalistic fortresses with spiritual "mental" detectors, cameras, and listening devices. God's desire is that our homes be dedicated to God and inhabited by people dedicated to God. If so, they will be filled with joy, love, peace, and light—the abundant life He promised.

In the book of *Nehemiah*, a report had come to Nehemiah in exile about the sad condition of Jerusalem; that the gates had been burned. There was great distress in the city because looters, prostitutes, thieves, swindlers, and murderers were running free. They had permission to be there because there was no gate or safeguards to keep them out.

Nehemiah was determined to rebuild. Against enemies, setbacks, and personal attacks, he did it. Once the walls and gates were back in place, he brought Ezra, a priest, to begin transforming the *inside* of the city by speaking to its inhabitants.

Ezra stood on the platform in full view of all the people. When they saw him open the book, they all rose to their feet. They read from the Book of the Law of God and clearly explained the meaning of what was being read, helping the people understand each passage. (Nehemiah 8:5, 8 NLT)

God has put His Word in the hearts of those who have put their faith in Him. Now His inner presence empowers them to guard the gates of their homes and lives.

And now, dear brothers and sisters, one final thing. Fix your thoughts on what is true, and honorable, and right, and pure, and lovely, and admirable. Think about things that are excellent and worthy of praise. (Philippians 4:8 NLT)

God has done His part in our lives through His grace. Our part is to move forward in faith through obedience to the Holy Spirit. Here's a simple faith pledge:

- I will be a watchman.
- I will guard the gates of my life.
- I will guard the gates of my home.
- I will proclaim and live God's word within and outside my gates.

This is the way to the freedom of the abundant life!

No Fear

Fear is a marketable commodity. There once was a television show, *The Fear Factor*, which cashed in on getting a contestant to do something that nobody in his right mind would do. News programs strike fear into our hearts with reports of terrorism, missing persons, random shootings, identity theft. Commercials get us to fear burglaries, falling and not being able to get up, side effects from drugs, and more.

Psychologists have coined names for hundreds of phobias. Here are a few:

- Peladophobia - Fear of bald people.
- Bufonophobia - Fear of toads.
- Pocrescophobia - Fear of gaining weight.
- Venustraphobia - Fear of beautiful women.
- Lutraphobia - Fear of otters.
- Arachibutyrophobia - Fear of peanut butter sticking to the roof of the mouth. (Really?)
- Phobophobia - Fear of phobias.
- Panophobia - Fear of everything.

There is rational fear that keeps us from injury or death, but we tend to have many irrational fears that can be crippling. Psychologists and marketers take advantage of our fears, and so does Satan. If he can cause a Christian to focus on fears, he can reduce that believer's effectiveness.

The Christian community has its fear-promoters, as well. Some preachers talk about losing your salvation, committing the unpardonable sin, bringing curses on yourself, making God angry with you, ending up in hell if you don't confess and repent of every sin, losing financial stability if you don't tithe, and many more.

Only God has a cure for fear. He has given us the Holy Spirit to pour out His love into our hearts. When we believe His love is perfect and eternal, it has tremendous power to set us free from fear.

There is no fear in love; but perfect love casts out fear because fear involves torment. But he who fears has not been made perfect in love. (1John 4:18 NKJV)

Fear is mentioned four times in the above verse. It is the Greek word, *phobos*, the root of our word, "phobia." It means "an irrational persistent fear or dread." The key word here is *irrational*. In Christ, however, our minds become rational.

Therefore I remind you to stir up the gift of God [His Spirit] *which is in you through the laying on of my hands. For God has not given us a spirit of fear* [irrational], *but of power and of love and of a sound mind* [rational]. *(2Timothy 1:6-7 NKJV)*

Fear is not created by the world around us, but by the way our minds respond to the world around us. It is based on what we *think* might happen in spite of all our supposed safeguards. For example, a man may have an insurance policy but still fear hurricanes. A woman may have a spouse but continue to fear that he may leave her alone. A family may have a security system but still fear a break-in by someone who won't be intimidated by it. It's good to have these things, but they should never be our sources of confidence. None of them can free us from fear.

Fear is the result of trusting in ourselves or in something besides God to deal with the challenges of life. Remember, *he who fears has not been made perfect in love.* When we have an irrational fear, it indicates that we still have more to learn about the greatness of God's love for us.

Even in the Old Testament in *Psalm 121, Isaiah 43* and many other scriptures, God promises His divine presence and protection. In the New Covenant, Paul said, *"Since I know it is all for Christ's good, I am quite content with my weaknesses and with insults, hardships, persecutions, and calamities. For when I am weak, then I am strong." (2Corinthians 12:10 NKJV)*

All through the Bible God promises that we have nothing to fear because of His great love and power.

We are children of the King, God Almighty Himself. He never loses sight of us. He never stops watching over us. But He does it His way. We have to trust that He knows what is best for us. When we fear there's only one place to go:

Come close to God, and God will come close to you. (James 4:8 NLT)

It's easy to get close to someone when you know that person loves you. That's the source of faith and power over our fear. His perfect love throws fear out of our minds. With His strong arm around us, what do we have to fear?

To those of you who have been born again, Jesus says, "Fear not! I am with you and will never leave you. What can anyone do to you? How can any circumstance drag you down? How can any sickness destroy the divine health I have placed in you? The worst anything the world can do is kill your body, and then you will be with Me for eternity. Obey My Spirit. Have respect and reverence for the Father's great power and authority that He shares with you. And you will never be afraid. Your joy will be full!"

"Obedience" Is A Four-Letter Word

The New Covenant of grace provides all believers in Christ with miraculous freedom from the law's condemnation. There's freedom from sin, guilt, fear, doubt. There is eternal forgiveness for all who believe the gospel and are born again of the Spirit.

However, if this is all we learn about grace we might conclude that grace is an excuse to sin, an opportunity to freely indulge our weaknesses and lusts. If we act on that wrong impression, we put ourselves back in slavery to sin.

The Bible never condones that kind of thinking:

Well then, since God's grace has set us free from the law, does that mean we can go on sinning? Of course not!

Don't you realize that you become the slave of whatever you choose to obey? You can be a slave to sin, which leads to death, or you can choose to obey God, which leads to righteous living. (Romans 6:15-16 NLT)

Note that receiving God's grace includes obedience that leads to righteous living. But when we hear the word *obedience*, our minds can miss God's grace and see Him as a law-giver who's watching every move we make, and if we mess up He's quick to whack us with a big stick.

The New Covenant of grace through Christ provides God's favor without the demands of obedience to any law. Christ has fulfilled all the law on our behalf. However, it's important to recognize that there is still a dimension of obedience in grace—not obedience to the law, but to what we believe.

For example, let's say you decide to go skydiving (this is you, not me!). At 10,000 feet the moment of truth comes. Everyone in the plane stands and prepares to jump. At the door, you hesitate. The leader asks, "Do you believe your parachute will open?" You say, "Yes." He says, "Okay, then, jump!" Still, you hesitate. "He says again, "Do you believe?" Again you say, "Yes," but you don't go out the door.

The point is that to believe includes action—obedience to what we believe. While our acts of obedience don't buy us favor, they do prove our faith is real—they are visible evidence of what we really believe. If we don't act on our belief—such as in our skydiving example—then others can rightly say, "I doubt that he really believes." As the book of *James* says, "Faith without action is dead."

A church sign in our neighborhood once said, "Jesus is not a law-giver but a life-giver." In the New Covenant God doesn't give us a revised set of regulations to obey, but a guide to the abundant life promised by Jesus.

I'm persuaded that God's first priority is to encourage His children to enter into the abundant life; to have a rich and satisfying life on this earth. Here are a few God's New Covenant encouragements:

- Love others as Jesus has loved you.
- Rejoice always.
- Pray without ceasing.
- Live by the Spirit and not by the flesh
- Come to the throne of grace to find help when needed.
- Present your bodies a living sacrifice.
- Don't conform to the world but be transformed by changing the way you think.
- Submit to God, resist the Devil
- Flee sexual immorality.

And the list goes on. Again, these are not laws. If we hear them that way we will inevitably fall back into condemnation because we can't possibly do everything perfectly all the time. Instead, we could say it this way, "If you believe you have become the righteousness of Christ, as He promised, then this is what your life will look like."

These encouragements are intended to illustrate the behavior of those whose nature is Christ. Their purpose is to reveal who we truly are—the righteousness of God in Christ. If we fail in these areas, our response should not be self-condemnation and pleading with God for forgiveness. No, our response should be, "That behavior does not reflect who I am. I repent, change my mind and direction, and with God's help will wash it from my life."

These encouragements lead us, day by day, into a rich, full, and satisfying relationship with the living God. They rescue us from any measure of slavery to sin. Then, as we enter into that abundant life, we are better able to communicate the love and power of God to others.

Who would be persuaded about God's grace from a person with a sinful lifestyle? Who would believe us about God's promises if there is no evidence of their fulfillment in us?

Others will be drawn to Jesus as they see Him revealed in us. So *obedience* is a four-letter word: *love*. I obey because of His love for me and my love response to Him. God's kind of love eliminates the need for a burdensome set of commands and requirements. While disobedience will never bring condemnation from God, obedience to His New Covenant encouragements will always result in the abundant life Jesus promised.

On Being Offended

One thing that's really hard to avoid in this life is being offended. In fact, this one thing destroys unity in churches more than anything else. People who are offended become spiritual vagabonds, going from church to church, collecting offenses as souvenirs and spreading trouble.

Jesus had very clear words and advice about being offended.

Then He said to the disciples, "It is impossible that no offenses [temptations to sin] should come, but woe to him through whom they do come! It would be better for him if a millstone were hung around his neck, and he were thrown into the sea, than that he should offend one of these little ones.

Take heed to yourselves. If your brother sins against you, rebuke him; and if he repents, forgive him. And if he sins against you seven times in a day, and seven times in a day returns to you, saying, 'I repent,' you shall forgive him."

And the apostles said to the Lord, "Increase our faith." (Luke 17:1-5 NKJV)

I can hear the disciples saying, "You've got to be kidding! Nobody has enough faith to do that!" Yes, the apostles understood, from experience, their inability to deal with offenses. Jesus was teaching them not to offend or to be offended. Both actions miss the mark. Neither is compatible with our identity in Christ. To offend means cause to sin, ensnare, or to lay a trap.

When *we offend others*, particularly if the person we offend is weak, he may stumble and sin by being offended, angry, perhaps vindictive. When *we are offended*, gossip starts, our hearts are hardened, others pick up the offense, and then there is stumbling and division among brethren.

The Bible is clear about the effects of offense.

An offended friend is harder to win back than a fortified city. Arguments separate friends like a gate locked with bars. (Proverbs 18:19 NLT)

And again, in the words of Jesus, *"Woe to the world because of offenses! For offenses must come, but woe to that man by whom the offense comes!" (Matthew 18:7 NKJV)* So—while it is impossible for us to avoid occasions to offend and be offended, God's grace makes it possible for us to handle them and keep the unity of the Spirit.

A person easily offended is either a *new* Christian, just learning, or a *weak* Christian who could have learned, but refused and remains selfish. The weak—the selfish— are easy to spot. They say things like, "The Pastor didn't greet me, someone sat in my chair, nobody read my prayer request, I'm not being fed, I don't like the worship" (It's not for you, by the way), they didn't invite me to the party, I was treated unfairly," and on it goes.

It's pretty clear that not only to offend is wrong, but to *be* offended is also wrong. When you take offense it's not your Spirit that's offended, it's your flesh. Flesh reactions cut off the flow of the Spirit for two reasons:

- Our focus goes from God to self.
- Pride rises up and humility fades away.

"Look what they did, said, to *me*!" Joy is diminished, bitterness grows, attitude deteriorates, and conversation dwells on how badly we were treated. We can only think of how insensitive and uncaring people are, how many hypocrites there are in church, etc. People will avoid us when we dwell on our offenses.

The result? We can't praise, can't worship, can't pray with a pure heart. We may even experience sickness, distress, depression, and more.

Ephesians 4:30 tells us that we grieve the Holy Spirit when we condemn and complain. Our words fail to impart grace to those who are listening.

1Thessalonians 5:19 tells us that it's possible for us to quench the Holy Spirit, to become a "wet blanket" that reduces the fire of the Spirit in our lives.

Acts 7:51 warns that we can resist the Spirit; we can become stubborn and deaf to what the Spirit wants to accomplish through His mercy and grace.

This is why an offended person is like a strong tower, locked behind steel bars. To hold an offense puts us in prison, while grace sets us free. To be offended doesn't line up with our new identity in Christ.

You were cleansed from your sins when you obeyed the truth, so now you must show sincere love to each other as brothers and sisters. Love each other deeply with all your heart. (1Peter 1:22 NLT)

Remember—it's our *flesh* that is offended, and because of that we can grieve, quench, and resist the Spirit of God.

Being offended is *always* wrong. We must never embrace it. The Holy Spirit will show us our need to forgive and get over it. He encourages us to let it go and empowers us through grace to do it. In Christ, *restoration* is always the goal. We must resist trying to vindicate ourselves, take revenge, get an apology, or condemn another.

If it is possible, as much as depends on you, live peaceably with all men. (Romans 12:18 NKJV) Do all that you can to live in peace with everyone. (Ibid. NLT)

It's important to note that this is something we *do* in obedience to the Spirit. Yes, offenses must come, but God's grace is always there to strengthen us and help us overcome their negative effect on our lives and ministries.

Simplicity In Prayer

Children pray interesting prayers. Here are a couple of examples: "Lead us not into temptation, but deliver us some E-mail."

"Dear God, thank you for the baby brother, but what I prayed for was a puppy."

"Lord, if you can't make me a better boy, it's okay. I'm having a real good time like I am."

I might have prayed that last one right up to the time I got saved. Anyway, we know prayer is good. It is powerful. It can change things—and us. However, the topic is overworked and, in many ways, gone wild. I don't have the "Seven Secrets Of Prayer Power." I don't have the final word. I have one word, "simplicity."

In *2Kings 5* there is the delightful story of Naaman, a high-ranking Syrian officer who had leprosy. A Jewish slave girl suggested he go see the prophet Elisha for the healing of his disease. So, Naaman packed his chariot with gold, silver, and other valuables to pay Elisha for his healing services. He arrived at the prophet's house with great expectations.

And Elisha sent a messenger to him, saying, "Go and wash in the Jordan seven times, and your flesh shall be restored to you, and you shall be clean."

But Naaman became furious, and went away and said, "Indeed, I said to myself, 'He will surely come out to me, and stand and call on the name of the LORD his God, and wave his hand over the place, and heal the leprosy.'

Are not the Abanah and the Pharpar, the rivers of Damascus, better than all the waters of Israel? Could I not wash in them and be clean?" So he turned and went away in a rage. (2 Kings 5:10-12 NKJV)

The story continues, and Naaman finally did as Elisha said and was healed. But let's go back and consider what he expected from Elisha. He said, "He'll come out to me, call out to God, wave his hand over my leprosy, and I'll be healed." Naaman was expecting quite a dramatic show. All he got was a very simple word—and it worked!

Jesus followed the same method as He went about miraculously healing people. It's amazing how easily it would happen. One of my favorite healing stories is that of a paralyzed man who was lowered down to Jesus from a hole in the roof of a house where Jesus was ministering to a large crowd.

When the man reached the floor, Jesus stood, called out to God, waved His hands over the man, and called on the choir to sing *Amazing Grace*. Not quite. That kind of thing happens in many healing meetings in today's church, and I'm not saying it's wrong.

My point here is that to bring healing, *Jesus turned to the paralyzed man and said, "Stand up, pick up your mat, and go home!" (Mark 2:10-11 NLT)* And that's exactly what happened! Now that's a simple prayer—a powerful example of His authority over the man's disability.

While teaching on prayer, Jesus said, *"When you pray, don't babble on and on as the Gentiles do. They think their prayers are answered merely by repeating their words again and again. (Matthew 6:7 NLT)* When I was a church pastor, people would come to me for prayer. If my prayer wasn't long, emotional, and loud they felt like I didn't really care. I've since learned that long, involved prayers are not necessary to produce results.

Jesus didn't have an unfair prayer advantage as the Son of God because He willingly set His glory aside to be our human example. Jesus' effectiveness came from an intimate relationship with the Father. That same relationship is available to everyone who is born again. Let's look at some Biblical prayer principles.

Jesus taught on prayer in *Matthew 6*, but after that, we never hear Him praying the "Lord's Prayer." In fact, there's no Biblical record of anyone else praying it, either. That's because once a believer is filled with the Holy Spirit and has become one with Christ, he has the potential of a much more powerful prayer life. You can pray the Lord's Prayer if you wish, but let me encourage you to tap the greater power of prayer that Jesus in us can produce. Develop your relationship with the Father.

Jesus never prayed Scripture in the sense of reminding the Father of His promises, or as leverage to get prayers answered. But today there are conferences and books that encourage us to do just that. Let's move beyond the superficial into the supernatural.

In *Mark 5* and *Luke 8* is the story of a man named Jairus who came to Jesus for help because his daughter was dying. It's interesting that Jesus never prayed that the doctors and nurses at the local Children's Hospital would be blessed and directed in their treatment of her. Again, there's nothing wrong with taking that approach, but I fear that we may miss out on the awesome opportunity to directly intercede in the power of the Holy Spirit.

While Jairus was still talking to Jesus, some men came from his home and told him his daughter had died. *But when Jesus heard what had happened, he said to Jairus, "Don't be afraid. Just have faith, and she will be healed." (Luke 8:50)* And she was!

This simple method of praying for healing was continued by Jesus' disciples. The apostles Peter and John encountered a man who had been lame from birth. He sat begging every day at the temple gate. Peter went up to him and said, *"I don't have any silver or gold for you. But I'll give you what I have. In the name of Jesus Christ the Nazarene, get up and walk!" (Acts 3:6 NLT)* And he did! They simply exercised the authority given to them—and every believer—by God.

I can't teach you the "secrets" of prayer. There are no secrets for children of God. We have Him, and He teaches us what we need to know. Paul said, *"Yes, everything else is worthless when compared with the priceless gain of knowing Christ Jesus my Lord. I have discarded everything else, counting it all as garbage, so that I may have Christ." (Philippians 3:8 NLT)*

Prayer power comes from *knowing* Him and knowing who we are in Him. It comes out of an intimate relationship, just as it was with Jesus. Remember the K.I.S.S. principle? "**K**eep **I**t **S**imple, **S**aints."

The Real Love Boat

The television series *The Love Boat* was a study in human romantic experiences and not all of them were pleasant or predictable. It was a fun comedy, and there was always a happy ending, but we know that happy endings don't always happen in human love life.

What kind of love have you experienced? As most people in our culture, I had been trained to believe in a certain kind of love. This training came from movies, songs, magazines, novels, psychology, family, friends, school, lover's lane, and whatever.

That love was usually shallow, emotional, unstable, or insecure. I was blown about by every wind of teaching on love. Love was something you fell into and out of, depending on circumstances.

When you say, "I love you because you make me feel good, or wanted, or important," that's not you loving her, that's you loving *you*. In this kind of relationship, you expect the other to do everything possible to keep you happy, and vice versa. You're both trying to mold one another into someone who fits your idea of the perfect companion.

However, that emotional environment isn't stable. If love is you keeping the other happy, then you must be on guard and not show any weakness. And if a weakness should be revealed, and it's pointed out to you, what's your natural defense? To comment on *the other's* weaknesses.

When the other person fails to keep you happy, satisfied, or content, you might say, "I've fallen out of love. Maybe someone else would be better." Or you connect with another person and Cupid hits you with an arrow and you say, "I don't love my spouse anymore; I love that other person now." This is a vicious cycle. But it's how the world defines love, and many Christians have been conditioned to define it that way, too.

The English language is unable to express the various dimensions of love. For example, the Greek of the New Covenant uses many different words translated "love." One expresses brotherly love, another expresses sexual love, still another expresses God's unique love. But in English, we say, "I love tacos," or, "I love my dog." Then we say, "I love my wife (or husband)" and it takes on the same shallow meaning. This world's view of love is, of course, inferior to God's love which is intensely personal, unconditional and eternal. The key to experiencing His love is, first of all, to be born again, and then to come to a Biblical understanding of His love nature. Then we can love others with true Biblical love.

We love each other because he loved us first. (1John 4:19 NLT)

If we think of God's love as being the same as the world's version of love, we'll see His love as conditional and dependent on our behavior. Then if we don't perform properly, we think He won't love us. And if God doesn't make *me* happy, I won't be motivated to love Him and may try some other spiritual or psychological approach.

God's version of love is so much better than the world's. When we're at our worst, He says, "Yeah, that's pretty bad, but I love you the same as ever and I'm not giving up on you." Here's probably the most-quoted scripture verse in the Bible. Let's look at it carefully for some real encouragement.

*For God **so** loved **the world** that **He gave** His only **begotten Son**, that **whoever believes in Him** should not **perish** but have everlasting* [eternal] *life. (John 3:16 NKJV)*

"So" is an intensity so great that we can't even imagine it.

"The world" means all of its inhabitants.

"He gave" tells us that God initiated this love—we didn't. He *so* loved all people that He reached out to us in our wicked, evil state. While we were still sinners, Christ died for us.

The *"begotten son"* was not *born* as one of God's kids, but was *begotten*—made up of the same substance as God Himself.

"Whoever believes in Him," tells us the invitation is open to everyone with no exceptions. It also tells us that our own efforts to be good will never make us good enough. "Believing" is the key to righteousness.

To believe is not an intellectual thing. It is to *know* that Jesus is who He says He is (God); has done what He says He did (died, rose from the dead, ascended into heaven; washed away all sin and offers us His righteousness); and will fulfill all what He says He will do (daily provide abundant life and one day take us to be with Him eternally).

God loves us just the way we are. We might think He will love some future version of us better, when we improve, when we get our act together, or when we get rid of some of our bad behavior. But Jesus sets us free from all that doubt the moment we believe.

"Perish" means to remain dead in sin—a broken life now and death forever.

"Eternal life" is quality now and quantity forever.

If we believed and were born again, then we have declared victory over the sin in our lives. We then become determined to mature in our faith so we can be true disciples, making a difference in the lives of others for the Kingdom of God. If this is not true of us, then perhaps we don't truly believe. It's serious business.

Let's abandon the world's idea of love and embrace God's. We can do it because God has given us His love.

Therefore, since we have been made right in God's sight by faith, we have peace with God because of what Jesus Christ our Lord has done for us.

Because of our faith, Christ has brought us into this place of undeserved privilege where we now stand, and we confidently and joyfully look forward to sharing God's glory.

We can rejoice, too, when we run into problems and trials, for we know that they help us develop endurance.

And endurance develops strength of character, and character strengthens our confident hope of salvation.

And this hope will not lead to disappointment. For we know how dearly God loves us, because he has given us the Holy Spirit to fill our hearts with his love. (Romans 5:1-5 NLT)

Welcome to the *real* love boat, where Jesus is the Captain. Everyone aboard will experience real love and a happy ending that has no end!

The Rating Game

Let's play the rating game. Rate your relationship with God on a scale of 1 to 10 where 10 is perfect and 1 is very weak.

Before reading on, put your rating number here: _____

Next, answer the question, "Why that number?" Here are some answers I've heard:

6 – I haven't been reading my Bible much lately.

2 – I got drunk after saying I'd never do it again.

9 – I just got back from a church service where I went to the altar and repented of all my sins.

Most people will rate their relationship with God on the basis of human understanding. The criteria are usually good or bad behavior, feelings of intimacy, or some other physical or emotional measurement. This mindset is produced when we feel we have violated—or have successfully obeyed—some legal requirement.

In order to rate a relationship, we need to know what a "relationship" is. Here are the dictionary definitions:

1. The state of being connected or related.
2. Association by blood or marriage; kinship.
3. The mutual dealings, connections, or feelings that exist between two parties, countries, people, as in a "business relationship."
4. An emotional or sexual affair.

In defining our relationship with God we probably wouldn't choose three or four. The definitions that come closest are one and two. But it's even greater than those. According to scripture, we are one with Christ, have been born into God's family, were washed clean by His blood, and are the bride of Christ. This is a totally integrated relationship. It could not be closer.

In the New Covenant of grace, Jesus' blood washed away all sin; past, present, and future. Our behavior failings—sins—have been dealt with and cannot damage our relationship with God. Paul states this truth very clearly:

... anyone who belongs to Christ has become a new person. The old life is gone; a new life has begun!

And all of this is a gift from God, who brought us back to himself through Christ. And God has given us this task of reconciling people to him. For God was in Christ, reconciling the world to himself, no longer counting people's sins against them. And he gave us this wonderful message of reconciliation. (2Corinthians 5:17-19 NLT)

God is righteous and holy and cannot dwell in the presence of sin, so the issue of our sin had to be dealt with once and for all by the death of Jesus Christ. *(See Hebrews 7:27; 9:26-28; 1Peter 3:18)* When God looks at us, He does not see our sin but the perfection of His Son. We have a new life—His. He will no longer count any of our sins against us.

What is your image of God? Loving Father or angry judge? Held in His arms or seated in His courtroom? Do you hear words of encouragement or words of judgment? Do His eyes reflect love and affirmation or do they instill fear? Is God celebrating your life or pointing out your failures?

It is our tendency to become like the God we worship. If we worship a God who is a loving Father, we will be confident in His love and reflect His love to others. If we see Him as an angry judge, we will be sin conscious, feel condemned, and hold others to the standards to which we are trying to live.

In *Romans 7:17-25* Paul teaches that sin dwells in our flesh; in our thoughts and the demands of our physical bodies. But sin cannot dwell in our Spiritual identity in Christ, so our relationship with God cannot be shaken. While we have been fully sanctified in Christ, the fullness of it is still being worked out in the physical realm.

No power in the sky above or in the earth below—indeed, nothing in all creation will ever be able to separate us from the love of God that is revealed in Christ Jesus our Lord. (Romans 8:39 NLT)

All three members of the Godhead have promised that nothing can ever change our relationship.

Father: In *Hebrews 13:5* God says He will never fail us, never abandon us.
Son: In *Matthew 28:20* Jesus said, *"I am with you always."*
Holy Spirit: And *John 14:16* says the Holy Spirit will never leave us.

So, our relationship with God is always a perfect ten, not by our feelings but because of our oneness with Him. We need to rate our relationship with God from His perspective, not ours. God isn't angry, does not demand performance, will never condemn us for anything we do. We are saved from the need to be saved by what we do or don't do—which is the curse of the law.

God's grace teaches us how to live righteously, yet many Christians try to live up to some code of conduct, believing that failure damages their relationship with God. That's bondage, not freedom, and Christ has made us free. Thank God we can trust that our relationship with God is always perfect. Thank God we can trust Him to work in us to transform us into the image of Christ.

A Herd Of Sacred Cows

I'm sure you've heard the expression, *sacred cow*, but maybe it's not really clear to you exactly what it means. The origin of that term is from India, where many believe that cows are an object of worship. Actually, the milk cow is not an object of worship but is *taboo*, which means no one is allowed to kill one. This taboo has strong religious roots, hence, *sacred*.

The word, *sacred*, is commonly used to describe something that is secure against violation, or immune from interference or change.

The Christian "religion" has rounded up a herd of sacred cows—traditions and beliefs that are zealously protected against attack. They are things we must not question or even suggest that they don't line up with the truth of the New Covenant.

These cows give out their milk to faithful church attendees. These folks have been raised on milk. They are used to milk. They like milk. They are not interested in meat. They may be born again, but they remain as children, with stunted growth because of their diet, content to remain in the confines of the barn. They say, "Let's invite some more children to come and drink milk with us."

Now don't get angry with me for what I just wrote, because the Bible says the same thing.

"You have been believers so long now that you ought to be teaching others. Instead, you need someone to teach you again the basic things about God's word. You are like babies who need milk and

cannot eat solid food. For someone who lives on milk is still an infant and doesn't know how to do what is right. Solid food is for those who are mature, who through training have the skill to recognize the difference between right and wrong." (Hebrews 5:12-14 NLT)

God forbid that we should ever eliminate one of our sacred cows. Those who tend the cows and dispense the milk guard the cow pen jealously. If the children were ever weaned off milk they might learn to feed themselves on nutritious food and experience freedom outside the barn.

They say, "We need the children to maintain the barn. We need them to participate in activities to entertain themselves and others. We need them to provide resources to keep the barn operating. We need to keep the children happy and occupied so they won't look outside the barn and be tempted to wander."

A sacred cow is any teaching that is obsolete, distorted, or imposed wrongly on God's people. Paul wanted believers to grow up, to mature, to experience true freedom.

Dear brothers and sisters, when I was with you I couldn't talk to you as I would to spiritual people. I had to talk as though you belonged to this world or as though you were infants in Christ. I had to feed you with milk, not with solid food, because you weren't ready for anything stronger. And you still aren't ready, for you are still controlled by your sinful nature (Gr. flesh). You are jealous of one another and quarrel with each other. Doesn't that prove you are controlled by your sinful nature (Gr. flesh)? Aren't you living like people of the world? (1 Corinthians 3:1-3 NLT)

It's test time. What is your emotional response when I name what I believe are some sacred cows in the church today?

- Denominationalism
- Tithing
- The Ten Commandments
- The Lord's Prayer
- The "Sinner's Prayer"

- The Altar and the Altar Call
- Communion (as usually practiced in church meetings)
- And there are many more.

If you feel protective of these traditions, that's normal. I used to teach many of them as sacred and beyond question. After all, they're in the Bible—well, many of them are. But I've discovered that the finished work of the cross has provided every born-again believer with much greater power and freedom than these traditions and practices provide.

Many sacred cows are Old Testament "shadows" of the superabundant grace life that God intends for His New Covenant people, the church. Multitudes of church-attending Christians are quite comfortable with sacred cows, and those who are truly saved will go to heaven when they die. But they may be missing out on the full and satisfying life Jesus said we could have on this side of heaven. The apostle Paul wrote, *"Christ has truly set us free. Now make sure that you stay free, and don't get tied up again in slavery to the law." (Galatians 5:1 NLT)*

Let me encourage you to examine the carefully protected traditions in the church. Are these truly New Covenant principles, or are they carry-overs from Old Testament law? Could some of them even be man-made traditions? Do they line up with the finished work of Christ on the cross? Are they fully compatible with the New Covenant of grace? *(See Acts 20:24)*

I'm certainly not suggesting you abandon your church fellowship. But I am suggesting you become like the Bereans, who searched the scriptures to find out if what they were being taught was really true. *(See Acts 17:10-11)*

God's desire is that we all experience the life and freedom that Jesus promised. That might mean letting go of some sacred-cow milk and adding some meat to our diet. As the Chick-fil-A cows say, "Eat Mor Chikin."

The Caravan Is On Its Way!

One of my favorite quotes is, "Experience is what you get when you were expecting something else." There are times in our Christian lives when God surprises us. He may change direction, bring something into our lives that we didn't expect, want, or care about. He may allow something we cherish to be removed to make room for His plan. He might put us in places or situations that we would never choose for ourselves.

Genesis 37 tells the story of Joseph, Jacob's (Israel's) son. God had far-reaching plans for Joseph, plans about which he had no clue.

At seventeen, Joseph was Jacob's favorite son. Jacob made him a beautiful, one-of-a-kind coat and allowed him to wear it around in front of the other brothers. Jacob would excuse Joseph from working while his brothers toiled in the fields. Joseph sat in the shade sipping his lemonade. Life was good, but his brothers resented him fiercely.

Comment: Just because you have the Father's favor, and the Father loves you and gives you gifts, doesn't mean others will like you.

God was also giving Joseph dreams about the future. They suggested that he would be in a position of authority and his brothers would bow down to him. He told his brothers about the dreams, and that just fanned the flames of resentment.

Comment: If God gives you prophetic vision and interpretation of dreams, you may not be popular.

Perhaps you feel blessed and at ease, and are expecting everything to continue smoothly. Joseph had no warning from God that things were about to change. As he was thinking, "This is good, this is working," events were beginning to move in a direction that would yank Joseph out of his blessed lifestyle.

One day Jacob sent Joseph out to find his brothers and check to see if they were okay. When he found them, their angry resentment rose up and they threw him into a pit. You expect that of your enemies, but of your brothers? Joseph might have wondered, "Is this God's way of blessing me—in a pit? I thought I was highly favored."

Comment: It doesn't matter how deep the pit is. There's not a devil in hell who can keep you in the pit when God wants you somewhere else.

Look at it this way. While he was in the pit, his brothers couldn't do anything more to him. They simply sat down to eat, enjoying their control over the thorn in their flesh. However, before they could act on their plan to murder Joseph, something happened. A caravan of Ishmaelite traders from Gilead came along and the brothers decided to make a profit and sell Joseph to them. He would be gone for good.

So Joseph was sold and traveled with a caravan going to Egypt. That caravan came along just exactly when God planned it. The caravan was on *God's* schedule. With God, timing is everything. It wasn't the Ishmaelite's timing, not Joseph's or his brothers' timing, not chance or fate. It was *God's* timing.

So let's not get tired of doing what is good. **At just the right time** *we will reap a harvest of blessing if we don't give up.* (Galatians 6:9 NLT)

Let's look at Joseph's travels to meet his brothers. Jacob said, "Go check on your brothers in Shechem. " It was 60 miles from Hebron, Joseph's home, to Shechem. At Shechem, a man told Joseph his brothers had moved on to Dothan—another 20 miles. Joseph traveled about 80 miles on his mission, and when his brothers saw him they threw him into a pit and planned to kill him.

This is where the story becomes very encouraging. The caravan came from Gilead, about 40 miles from Dothan. Here's the schedule: When Joseph was about two-thirds of the way from Hebron to Shechem, God sent out a caravan from Gilead to Dothan.

Before Joseph needed the caravan, God sent it out! Before your problem ever surfaces, God gets the caravan moving. God puts it together and sends it out so it arrives exactly when it's needed. Jesus said, *"Your Father knows exactly what you need even before you ask him! (Matthew 6:8 NLT)*

The caravan carried God's provision, the right stuff from Gilead to meet Joseph's need.

Is there no balm in Gilead, is there no physician there? (Jeremiah 8:22 NKJV)

Gilead was known for its production of a balm, or ointment, that had powerful medicinal benefits. God sent what Joseph needed—emotional healing from the threat of death.

You or a loved one may be in a pit right now, with heartache, pain, and suffering. Listen for the hoof beats of the camels carrying what's needed. It will arrive exactly on time—from God's perspective, not yours.

Joseph was destined by God to be elevated to the second highest position in the world. Before all this happened, if someone had asked him, "Want to leave home and work for Pharaoh in Egypt?" He'd have probably said, "Are you kidding? I've got it made, and I'm obviously in God's will right where I am!"

Sometimes the only way God can get us where He wants us is by orchestrating events that are beyond our control. If we are in control of our situations, we're not likely to leave our comfort zones. God's strategy was not designed to make Joseph comfortable, but to get him where He wanted him to be. God took him from pit to palace, using the caravan to move him forward.

All was not easy in Egypt. He was falsely accused, thrown into prison and forgotten there for years. Eventually, he fulfilled his destiny. He was given the second most powerful position in Egypt, and in that position was able to save multitudes of people from starvation. In addition, he was finally reunited and reconciled with his brothers. When his brothers feared that Joseph would take revenge on them, he encouraged them by saying, *"You intended to harm me, but God intended it all for good. He brought me to this position so I could save the lives of many people. (Genesis 50:20 NLT)*

Whatever your situation may look like today, trust God—the caravan is on its way. And even greater things lie ahead!

The Trap Of Self-Righteousness

When someone begins bragging about spiritual or ministry accomplishments, it's a sign that a certain amount of self-righteousness has crept in. The simple definition of self-righteousness is the belief that my skills, position, or performance contribute to my right standing with God. And, since I believe this is true, I will have a tendency to talk about those accomplishments in order to gain the respect and admiration of others.

Self-righteousness is a blind and self-absorbed condition that can't be overcome by human effort. It fails to recognize that outside of Christ there is no real identity and no true righteousness.

Here are some of the struggles of the self-righteous:

- Self-consciousness; regretting poor performance and striving for visible success.
- Judgmental of others' performance and failures.
- Focused on how others perceive them; fear of rejection; a people-pleasing spirit.
- Sin consciousness; unhealthy focus on their own shortcomings and feeling condemned much of the time.

The alternative to self-righteousness is faith-righteousness. Paul clearly states, *"I no longer count on my own righteousness through obeying the law; rather, I become righteous through faith in Christ. For God's way of making us right with himself depends on faith."* (Philippians 3:9 NLT)

The principle of self- versus faith-righteousness is illustrated by Jesus when He said, *"On judgment day many will say to me, 'Lord!*

Lord! We prophesied in your name and cast out demons in your name and performed many miracles in your name.' [Look how well we performed.]

But I will reply, 'I never knew you. [We never had a relationship.] *Get away from me, you who break God's laws.'"* **(**Matthew 7:22-23 NLT)

These people were trying to earn right standing with God by their own efforts, obeying the law and doing good works. Jesus often taught that relationship trumps performance. Instead of striving to build our own strength, we must become dependent on *His* strength. Paul wrote, *"We now have this light shining in our hearts, but we ourselves are like fragile clay jars containing this great treasure. This makes it clear that our great power is from God, not from ourselves." (2Corinthians 4:7 NLT)*

The religious mind always defines righteousness in terms of knowing good and doing it, and knowing evil and avoiding it. This is eating from the tree of the knowledge of good and evil, which produces death. *(See Genesis 2:15-17)*

When we are born again, we need to change the way we define "sin." Self-righteousness thinks of sin in terms of violating a set of rules. It's not God's will for us to live a life full of sin-consciousness which produces guilt from our failures and a determination to try harder to do better. Our bad behavior dominates our minds, and we think that it's up to us to correct it.

For a believer, sin is unbelief; the refusal to believe that all our righteousness now comes only from Christ Himself. This sin does not condemn us but keeps us from enjoying our freedom in Christ. To overcome this unbelief, we must learn to live in obedience to the Holy Spirit. The Spirit points us to Jesus because our relationship with Him is always the key to seeing our behavior improve. Paul is very clear, *"I say then: Walk in the Spirit, and you shall not fulfill the lust of the flesh." (Galatians 5:16 NKJV)*

Note the progression: *First* we walk in the Spirit (relationship), *then* we won't give in to the lust of the flesh (performance).

In *Philippians 3* Paul says he sets aside all his impressive qualifications so that he can *know* Christ in all aspects of His life. He says he has not yet reached perfection, but he presses forward with determination, forgetting the past and looking toward what lies ahead. Paul here echoes Jesus in that instead of being conscious of our *performance*, it's our *relationship* with Christ that counts. It's *His* performance, not mine, that makes the difference.

Read *Philippians 3:8-14* to find Paul's principles for escaping self-righteousness. Here's my commentary:

1. **Count every asset a loss.** We add up all our talents, skills, education, position, influence, wisdom, and set them all aside. In our resulting weakness, God decides which of our abilities are to be used, and which new abilities He will develop in us.
2. **Count knowing Christ as the highest goal.** We get to know Him better through His Word, prayer, good teaching, and fellowship with other believers.
3. **Take *all* the life of Christ.** We embrace not only His power and perfection but also His suffering and rejection. We follow Him regardless of the circumstances. Paul said, in effect, "I want it all because anything less is not His life."
4. **Put the past behind and leave it there.** Forget the good and the bad; the accomplishments and failures. Live today in the righteousness of Christ that comes by faith. We don't *deny* the past—it really did happen. But we face it, learn from it, make amends and forgive, asking for God's help to truly let it all go. The goal is to move ahead, reaching forward and not dragging the weight of the past.

What, then, is the prize? We're not working to receive salvation because in Christ we already have it. The prize is Christ Himself; building a rich, intimate relationship with Him now and for eternity.

If our whole focus is to do good and avoid evil, our lives will be filled with frustration, failure, and disappointment. Oh, we'll get to heaven, but our self-righteousness will never be profitable. However, if our whole focus is on the grace of God and our relationship with Christ, we will live genuine, holy lives and will fulfill everything God has for us. Our lives will be full and joyful, even with all our struggles in the natural realm. Our relationships will be rich and meaningful, and our treasure in heaven will be great.

Are You Living In The Shadows?

Shadows give limited facts about reality. They *point* to reality but don't tell the whole story. In the photo below we know there are four, maybe five or six people. We don't know what sex they are, how they are dressed, how old they are, how tall they are—we know very little about them.

We must see the reality to understand the details of the shadow. And we must see Jesus to fully understand His grace.

So don't let anyone condemn you for what you eat or drink, or for not celebrating certain holy days or new-moon ceremonies or Sabbaths. For these rules are only shadows of the reality yet to come. And Christ himself is that reality. (Colossians 2:16-17 NLT)

The Old Testament laws were not the substance, but only the shadow of the reality to come—Jesus Christ. God first revealed Himself through natural "shadows" that pointed to a spiritual substance of faith, then to Jesus Himself as the full revelation of the Father. *(See Colossians 2:8-10)* All shadows from the Old Testament point to Jesus, His grace, and His light. Here are just a few examples:

The blood on the Israelites' doorposts in Egypt and the blood of animal sacrifices are shadows. The substance was Jesus' shed blood and its power to save and forgive. *(See Ephesians 1:6-8)*

When the Israelites in the wilderness were bitten by snakes, Moses put a bronze serpent on a pole that healed all who looked at it. This was a shadow of the healing power of Jesus in His atonement as He hung on the cross. *(See John 3:14-17)*

The temple priesthood in Israel was a shadow. The substance is the royal priesthood of believers and of Jesus as high priest always making intercession for us. *(See 1Peter 2:9; Hebrews 4:14; Romans 8:34)*

The various Temple buildings in Israel's history were shadows. The substance is the body of Jesus Christ, His church, and the reality of every believer being the Temple of the Holy Spirit. *(See Ephesians 2:19-22; 1Corinthians 6:19)*

In Psalm 23 David spoke of the valley of the shadow of death. This was not death itself, but only a shadow. The threat of death produces no fear in the believer, and the substance is eternal life in Christ. *(See 1Corinthians 15:54-58; John 3:16)*

The Ten Commandments and all the Law of Moses were only shadows of the substance. Jesus Christ has fulfilled all the law and we have now been given the righteousness of God in Christ. *(See Romans 10:4; Philippians 3:8-9)*

The tithe (the 10%+ tax) was also only a shadow. The substance is joyful generosity in giving without pressure and legalistic demands. The New Covenant teaches giving, not tithing. *(See 2Corinthians 9:7)*

There are innumerable shadows in the Old Testament. They were important, giving clues about reality when the reality couldn't yet be seen. The problem today? We forget that the shadows are not the reality, and impose these shadows on ourselves and on each other. We forget that Christ has set us free from the law of sin and death—from the shadows. *(See Romans 8:2)*

Many times Paul corrected those who were focusing on shadows of the Old Testament.

I am shocked that you are turning away so soon from God, who called you to himself through the loving mercy of Christ. You are following a different way that pretends to be the Good News but is not the Good News at all. You are being fooled by those who deliberately twist the truth concerning Christ. (Galatians 1:6-7 NLT)

Paul pleaded with the Galatian church, warning them against going back into the old legalistic system. He wrote, *"I plead with you to live as I do in freedom from these things, for I have become like you Gentiles—free from those laws." (Galatians 4:12)*

Religious church people still argue about the Sabbath, rituals, tithing, keeping the Ten Commandments, communion with wine or grape juice, unleavened bread or Wonder bread, women in pants or dresses, pastors in Hawaiian shirts or clerical collars, meetings in church buildings (temples) or houses, etc.

All of these and more are arguments about shadows. We do not live in the shadows of the law, we live in the light of Christ and the fullness of His grace. Paul wrote, *"… let us who live in the light be clearheaded, protected by the armor of faith and love, and wearing as our helmet the confidence of our salvation." (1Thessalonians 5:8 NLT)*

… God is light, and there is no darkness in him at all. So we are lying if we say we have fellowship with God but go on living in spiritual darkness; we are not practicing the truth. But if we are living in the light, as God is in the light, then we have fellowship with each other, and the blood of Jesus, his Son, cleanses us from all sin. (1John 1:5-7 NLT)

The substance, the spiritual reality of the Kingdom of Heaven took on human form. In Jesus Christ, flesh and Spirit came together; natural and spiritual reality combined, full of grace and truth. Since we are filled with the Holy Spirit, as He was, we are the substance of God's promise and plan fulfilled. We can say the same as Walter Brennan in the television series, *The Guns Of Will Sonnett*, "No brag, just fact!"

How To Discover The Will Of God

There is lots of misinformation about God's will for our lives. Multitudes of believers are afraid to make decisions; afraid they will step out of the will of God. The biggest misconception is that there are three levels to the will of God—His good will, His acceptable will, and His perfect will. We get this idea from an incorrect interpretation of this Bible verse:

*And do not be conformed to this world, but be transformed by the renewing of your mind, that you may prove what is that **good** and **acceptable** and **perfect** will of God. (Romans 12:2 NKJV)*

I don't believe there are "levels" to the will of God. Another translation makes it clear:

…you will learn to know God's will for you, which is good and pleasing and perfect. (Romans 12:2 NLT)

Rather than establishing three levels of God's will, this verse simply tells us how wonderful it is. Here are some thoughts on the will of God from the New Covenant perspective.

1. God's will is perfected in us through Jesus Christ.

The will of God is Jesus Christ in us. Another way of saying it is, "We believers *are* the will of God." When born from above, we receive the life of Christ. He lives in us and wants to express Himself through us.

This means His will is not something to be found, but to be fulfilled. Grace is all of God's power and none of mine. All I have to do is believe it and follow His direction.

God saved you by his grace when you believed. And you can't take credit for this; it is a gift from God. (Ephesians 2:8 NLT)

When we continually trust the Holy Spirit to guide us, we never need to feel anxious about God's will. It's not our job to figure out our lives, but to allow Jesus to live His life through us. This means we can relax and trust Him.

So when we feel anxious about a decision we must make, or if we desperately want to know God's will in a situation, our outlook needs to be, "My stress over this decision is not necessary. I can pray, relax, and make a decision without a lightning bolt or shout from God."

Paul writes, *"Don't worry about anything; instead, pray about everything. Tell God what you need, and thank him for all he has done. Then you will experience God's peace, which exceeds anything we can understand. His peace will guard your hearts and minds as you live in Christ Jesus."* (Philippians 4:6-7 NLT)

2. We have the mind of Christ.

"Who can know the LORD's thoughts? Who knows enough to teach him?" But we understand these things, for we have the mind of Christ. (1Corinthians 2:16 NLT)

When we live according to the Spirit our thoughts are guided by Jesus because he is in us. When confronted with a choice we can go ahead and make it in faith that He would make the same choice. I think when we cry out, "Lord, what do you want me to do?!" His answer might just be, "I want you to decide based on My life in you."

Basically, God's will is for Christ to live in us and express Himself through us as we live our lives. It's Christ in me and Christ through me. God is behind every door as we travel through life, even the door of sin. Sin isn't okay, but if we choose that door He goes with us because He is in us. His will, then, is to lead us back to where we should be.

There are times when God will give us clear direction, a word that will be clear and unambiguous. However, most of the time we are free to choose our path and not compelled to wait for God to open the door. This removes the fear of "missing" God's will.

We are free to marry any believing person without waiting for God to bring along just the "right" person. We are free to take any job that doesn't cause us to sin. We are free to live anywhere we want to. Our understanding of who we are in Christ will help us make good choices.

Shouldn't we pray about our decisions? Well, should we breathe to stay alive? Of course! Prayer, opportunities, and our desires all work together to guide us. Life isn't a thousand-piece jigsaw puzzle that brings frustration. Life is a beautiful painting that God reveals to us as we simply live and work and enjoy.

3. We should not second-guess His will once we've made a faith decision.

What causes us to second-guess our decisions? When things don't work out as we expected; when things are tougher that we thought. Let's say we choose to live on the beach to enjoy the ocean, the sun and tropical food. Then a hurricane comes along. We might think, "Oh, no! I must have missed God's will." No, God simply is working things out His way, never leaving us or forsaking us. He just chose not to tell us in advance about the hurricane. So, unpleasant or unexpected events do not indicate that we missed God's will.

What if I really do make an ungodly or selfish choice? God is bigger than our mistakes. He is right there with us and will continue to lovingly guide us through any mess we can create.

… God has said, "I will never fail you. I will never abandon you." (Hebrews 13:5 NLT)

[Jesus said,] *"I will ask the Father, and he will give you another Advocate, who will never leave you. He is the Holy Spirit, who leads into all truth. The world cannot receive him, because it isn't looking for him and doesn't recognize him. But you know him, because he lives with you now and later will be in you." (John 14:16-17 NLT)*

The issue of discovering God's will really is that simple. We are God's will, we have the mind of Christ, and we should not second-guess decisions if circumstances become unpleasant. Let's relax and let Him live His life *through* us, *as* us!

Power To Fly

For most of my life, I have been fascinated by airplanes. I do have a private pilot's license, but these days I fly only radio controlled models. My wife is pleased.

We are all aware that an airplane will never leave the ground unless power is applied by the engine, or another airplane tows it into the air, or it is launched by some other method. It's basically dead to its created purpose until some sort of power is applied to get it in the air. It may be beautiful to look at and worthy of admiration, but it's still dead to its purpose while on the ground.

We could say the same thing about a human being. Like an airplane, it is an intricate creation.

You [God] made all the delicate, inner parts of my body and knit me together in my mother's womb. Thank you for making me so wonderfully complex! Your workmanship is marvelous—how well I know it. (Psalm 139:13-14 NLT)

And *Ephesians 2:10* says we are God's masterpiece, or workmanship.

We could admire all the parts of the human body and marvel at its beautiful appearance and complex workings. However, as with the airplane, it is dead to its created purpose until power is applied. How can the human acquire power for living?

The answer is to receive the life of Christ, to believe that He is the only-begotten Son of God, that He died to pay the penalty for our sin, and that He lives to give us new life through His Holy Spirit.

The Spirit of God, who raised Jesus from the dead, lives in you. And just as God raised Christ Jesus from the dead, **he will give**

life to your mortal bodies *by this same Spirit living within you. (Romans 8:11 NLT)*

When we are born again, God's Holy Spirit takes up residence in our physical bodies, connecting us to all the power of the Kingdom of God. This provides both spiritual and physical life and power.

When an airplane flies, there two laws at work—the law of aerodynamics and the law of gravity. While flying under power, the law of aerodynamics keeps it in the air. But the law of gravity is always at work trying to bring it down. As long as the power is applied, gravity is defeated and it performs its created purpose. If it loses power, it will come down.

In our born-again lives, there are also two laws at work.

For the **law of the Spirit of life in Christ Jesus** *has made me free from the* **law of sin and death**. *(Romans 8:2 NKJV)*

The life of His Spirit within us provides all the power we need to soar like eagles. We overcome the law of sin and death—religious demands and condemnation—and fly far above the world, the flesh, and the devil. We are then equipped to demonstrate God's power and love to everyone and fulfill our created purpose.

We apply His power by faith, believing that no matter how hard the law of sin and death tries to bring us down we are free. We need not fear it or give in to its demands.

Have you not known? Have you not heard? The everlasting God, the Lord, The Creator of the ends of the earth, Neither faints nor is weary.

His understanding is unsearchable.

He gives power to the weak, And to those who have no might He increases strength.

Even the youths shall faint and be weary, and the young men shall utterly fall,

But those who wait on the Lord shall renew their strength;

They shall mount up with wings like eagles,

They shall run and not be weary,
They shall walk and not faint. (Isaiah 40:28-31NKJV)

This is the mark of a saint living a life empowered by the Spirit of God. God provides the desire in our hearts and the power to fulfill His will in the natural. We simply obey and act.

The work we do in the natural realm? Fly. Run. Walk. We won't burn out, rust out, run out of gas, or abandon the church. We don't go flat like a battery and need recharging. We are plugged into an eternal power supply. That is the law of the Spirit of life in Christ (the grace of God working in us) overcoming the law of sin and death (religious self-effort).

The eagle stands on the high place, spreads his wings, and the wind lifts him into the sky to begin his flight. His physical involvement was minimal. Spread your wings in faith and the wind of the Spirit will do the rest.

To Tithe Or Not to Tithe

There are many debates in the church. What words to say at baptism, how to receive communion, whether house churches are better than institutional churches, whether or not you can lose your salvation, whether or not speaking in tongues is for today—on and on. The reason we have debates is that there is more than one way to look at many of these issues. If we dig in our heels and refuse to budge, we'll never get closer to the truth. Both sides can't be completely right.

Money is a huge Biblical topic. There are some 2000 scripture verses that talk about it! I'm sure not going to debate the tens of thousands of pages that have been written on the use of money in the church.

When the apostle Paul wrote to Timothy about money he said, *"Now godliness with **contentment** is great gain. For we brought nothing into this world, and it is certain we can carry nothing out.*

*And having food and clothing, with these we shall be **content**.*

*But those who **desire** to be rich fall into temptation and a snare, and into many foolish and harmful **lusts** which drown men in destruction and perdition.*

*For the **love** of money is a root of all kinds of evil, for which some have strayed from the faith in their **greediness**, and pierced themselves through with many sorrows."* (1 Timothy 6:6-10 NKJV)

Note the words I've highlighted above. It's pretty clear that it isn't the *quantity* of money God addresses, but our *attitude* towards it. And when we get into animated and even angry arguments about money and "tithing" we have the wrong attitude and it causes division.

What about tithing? Well, under the law of Moses, tithing was basically an income tax, a legal requirement for the people to provide food for the priests, the Levites, and the poor. It was primarily groceries, not money. All the annual tithes together amounted to more than 20% of a person's produce or increase. Today's version of tithing is nothing like that. It's a closed system. Give exactly 10% of your income in cash and you have supposedly met God's minimum requirements.

Since the cross, we are no longer subject to the Old Testament law system. We have entered into the freedom of God's grace. Jesus Himself focused on generous giving rather than strict tithing. On one occasion He recognized the Pharisees for their faithful obedience in tithing. *(See Matthew 23:23-24)* They were faithful to follow the letter of the law as required, but Jesus was more focused on their bad attitude. His point was that they held to the letter of the law yet ignored the spirit of generosity. Not once does any New Covenant writer command believers to tithe. Generosity is the heart of New Covenant giving.

Giving as taught in the New Covenant is an open system where we don't measure what we give, but we are willing to give anything we have as God directs. In Jesus' words, *"Give, and you will receive. Your gift will return to you in full—pressed down, shaken together to make room for more, running over, and poured into your lap. The amount you give will determine the amount you get back."* (Luke 6:38 NLT)

It's much easier to tithe than to give. Many of us would rather obey a rule than to operate in freedom. Jesus pronounced "woes" on those legalistic leaders who focused on the tithe tax and neglected generous giving. I am certain that if churches would abandon the tithe tax and preach on giving the way Jesus did, there would be no lack of funds.

Bottom line, it's not "wrong" to tithe. What's wrong is for the church to teach that tithing is required and that a person will lose out in some way if he doesn't do it faithfully. That's a return to the Old Testament tithe tax.

Some say that tithing forms a foundation for future giving, or that it may be a good start for new believers. That explanation just sidesteps the real issue. It is born out of fear that the church organization won't have enough money to pay its bills. Again, I am sure that teaching New Covenant giving would provide an abundance of provision.

For the Kingdom of God is not a matter of what we eat or drink, [or whether or not we tithe] *but of living a life of goodness and peace and joy in the Holy Spirit. (Romans 14:17-19 NLT)*

Since I now understand that Jesus fulfilled all the law on my behalf I could not, in good conscience, teach that if a person doesn't tithe he's robbing God and will be cursed *(See Malachi 3:8-9)*. The truth is so much better:

But Christ has rescued us from the curse pronounced by the law. When he was hung on the cross, he took upon himself the curse for our wrongdoing. For it is written in the Scriptures, "Cursed is everyone who is hung on a tree." (Galatians 3:13 NLT)

In *Malachi 3:8-12* we find a curse for not tithing and a blessing for tithing. The New Covenant promises God's great blessing for giving generously and a smaller blessing for being stingy. But there are no curses. Here's the New Covenant way:

Remember this—a farmer who plants only a few seeds will get a small crop. But the one who plants generously will get a generous crop. You must **each make up your own mind** *as to how much you should give. Don't give reluctantly or in response to pressure. For God loves the person who gives cheerfully.*

*And God will generously provide all you need. Then you will always have **everything you need** and plenty **left over** to share with others. As the Scriptures say, "Godly people give generously to the poor. Their good deeds will never be forgotten." (2Corinthians 9:6-9 NLT)*

The temple was the storehouse for Old Testament tithing. Today there is no temple building. We are the temple and the storehouse. God has deposited great riches in our lives, and we are to dispense those riches to those in need and to ministries that bring glory to God.

The debate will go on until Jesus comes. But I do know this:

1. God wants us to love and trust in Him in all things, including money and other material possessions.
2. God wants us to hold everything we have loosely so that when He urges us to give it's not painful but cheerful.
3. God wants us to give as He gives—generously, without holding back even His best.

*For God so loved the world that He **gave** … (John 3:16 NKJV)*

Love Those Mountaintop Experiences!

We love "mountaintop experiences" in our Christian lives. These are times of emotional excitement, thrilling revelations, and great victories. God seems so near and so powerful. You want it to continue—you don't want to go home.

I used to read about Jesus' transfiguration in *Luke 9:28-36* and wonder, "What's that all about?" Now I know, and that understanding was an important milestone on my journey from law to grace. Here's the paraphrased story:

Jesus took Peter, James, and John up on a mountain. While praying, Jesus began to literally shine brightly like there was a light inside Him. Then Moses and Elijah appeared beside Him. They didn't shine. The disciples were sleeping, as they often did when Jesus was praying, and woke up to see a brilliant, shining Jesus with Moses and Elijah.

Peter (of course) said, "Wow! Let's build three memorial shelters and hang out up here with them." Just then a cloud appeared over them. God the Father's voice spoke from the cloud, "This is my Son, my Chosen One, listen to Him." Suddenly Moses and Elijah vanished and Jesus stood there alone.

The point?

- Moses represented the Law.
- Elijah represented the Prophets.
- Jesus represented the Father. *He who has seen Me has seen the Father... (John 14:9 NKJV).*

It's very clear that the Father's message to the disciples and to us today is that Jesus' words would supersede those of both the law and the prophets. Jesus said, *"Don't misunderstand why I have come. I did not come to abolish the law of Moses or the writings of the prophets. No, I came to accomplish their purpose* [to fulfill them]." *(Matthew 5:17 NLT)*

Jesus fulfilled the three Jewish Law systems:

- Ceremonial law—Jesus the final sacrifice.
- Judicial law—Jesus the righteous judge.
- Moral law—Jesus the sinless man.

Jesus fulfilled the Prophets:

- The coming of the Messiah—Jesus, the Messiah, has come.
- The judgment of sin—Jesus became sin and paid the full penalty for all sin.
- God dwelling in man—Jesus, Immanuel, inhabits us through the Holy Spirit.

Back on the mountaintop, when Moses and Elijah vanished the Father said, "From now on you listen to My Son, Jesus. He is your final authority." The Father set Jesus apart from and above the Law and the Prophets. Jesus was shining with the glory of God, full of grace and truth. *(See John 1:14-17 NKJV)*

"Until John the Baptist, the law of Moses and the messages of the prophets were your guides. **But now** *the Good News of the Kingdom of God is preached, and everyone is eager to get in. (Luke 16:16 NLT)*

Notice the words, *"but now"* in the above verse. The Law and the Prophets do not guide Christians. The Holy Spirit within us is our guide. The Law and the Prophets still have a voice, but only to unbelievers with the purpose of leading them to Christ. Once we are born again in Jesus, these systems have no power or authority over our lives.

People asked Jesus, "What should we do to do the works of God? Keep the big ten? Win the world for Jesus? Become a missionary? Do more good than bad? Come on, Jesus, tell us what to do!"

Jesus told them, "This is the only work God wants from you: Believe in the one he has sent." (John 6:29 NLT)

Don't we still ask the same question? And He still gives the same answer. Right away the devil comes along and says, "Did God really say, 'just believe?' No, that's not enough. You've got to do more, do better, try harder, stop sinning. Just do it!"

If we believe that, we become plagued with doubt and uncertainty. We wonder, "Have I done enough? Is what I have done acceptable? What should I do next? What should I stop doing? Is God mad at me? Will He punish me?" We fall back into a system of law, and instead of entering His rest we enter into restlessness.

If your spiritual foundation is any system of religious law, then you tend to focus on your sin and failings and the Bible is used to bring condemnation. Since religious law never made anyone righteous and gives power to sin, this foundation is built on shifting sand. It's a dead end. *(See Galatians 2:21; 1Corinthians 15:56)*

If your spiritual foundation is God's grace, then you focus on your righteousness in Christ, and the Bible is used to bring freedom and produce righteous living. The foundation of a true understanding of God's grace will always lead to righteous living, not to sinfulness. It will lead to productive activity, not to laziness or inactivity. So, if you're looking for a mountaintop experience, you're already there in Christ. Enjoy the ride—it's never boring.

What Are You Full Of?

My Mom was always able to see through my childhood deceptions. One day I came home late from school and told her an exaggerated story about getting lost on my way home, riding my bike for miles in uncharted territory, and finally following the neighbor's dog to the right street. My story was clever, and I told it with great conviction. I even believed it myself. With a raised eyebrow and hands on her hips, she replied, "You're full of beans!" From past experience, I knew this meant, "I don't believe a word of it!"

Anyway, we're all full of something. God made us to be containers. Under the old covenant of law, the Bible speaks of things people are full of:

To religious leaders, Jesus said, "... *inside you are full of hypocrisy and lawlessness." (See Matthew 23:27-28)*

James observes, "... *no man can tame the tongue. It is an unruly evil, full of deadly poison." (See James 3:7-9)*

Paul discerns a problem with Simon the sorcerer: "... *I see that you are full of bitterness and captive to sin."(See Acts 8:18-23)*

At a church potluck dinner, I was walking through a crowd with two full glasses of iced tea. A man suddenly stood up and knocked me off balance. A generous portion of iced tea went airborne, splashing on several bystanders, rendering me instantly unpopular.

The lesson? Whatever we're full of will spill on everyone around us when we're "bumped" in some way by life's events. If hypocrisy fills my life, I'm quick to put on an act in order to gain an advantage. If my tongue is full of poison, it will spill out when things don't go right. If I'm full of bitterness, anger will spill out and impact those nearby.

God wants us to be full of the same things that filled Jesus. John wrote of Him, *"And the Word became flesh and dwelt among us, and we beheld His glory, the glory as of the only-begotten of the Father, full of grace and truth." (John 1:14 NKJV)*

He was full of grace, the power of God, and truth, the Word of God. When we're born again and made new creatures in Christ, we are full of the same. Paul writes, *"Don't be drunk, filled with wine, because that will ruin your life. Instead, avoid excessive wine and let the Holy Spirit fill and control you. Then you will sing psalms and hymns and spiritual songs among yourselves, making music to the Lord in your hearts." (Ephesians 5:18-19 my paraphrase)*

Have you ever heard someone sing who's filled with wine? It may ruin *your* life, too. God gives us a new song of grace, inspired by the Holy Spirit, filling our hearts with music to the Lord. Since we're full of the Holy Spirit, *He* will spill out when we experience life's potholes, and those around us will be blessed.

Jesus once cried out to the crowds, *"If anyone thirsts, let him come to Me and drink* [be filled with the Holy Spirit]. *He who believes in Me, as the Scripture has said, out of his heart will flow rivers of living water* [he will spill life on everyone around him]." *(John 7:37-39 NKJV)*

What does "living water" look like? An analysis would reveal *love, joy, peace, patience, kindness, goodness, faithfulness, gentleness, and self-control. (See Galatians 5:22-23)* If we happen to be close to a Spirit-filled person when life gives him a nasty jolt, we'll be splashed with the fruit juice of the Spirit.

Stephen, an average church member, was full of the Holy Spirit, qualifying him to serve tables. But that's not all he did.

Now Stephen, a man full of God's grace and power, did great wonders and miraculous signs among the people. (Acts 6:8 NKJV)

The Holy Spirit brings God's grace and power, both of which are to be spilled out on those nearby.

Jesus' said, *"If you are filled with light, with no dark corners, then your whole life will be radiant, as though a floodlight is shining on you." (Luke 11:36 NLT)* It's a radiant life, like a floodlight, and the light of Jesus spills out all around us.

We are also filled with love, the very essence of God. Paul writes, *"Live a life filled with love, following the example of Christ. He loved us and offered himself as a sacrifice for us, a pleasing aroma to God." (Ephesians 5:2 NLT)*

Jesus had some good friends named Lazarus, Martha, and Mary, who lived in Bethany, a town outside Jerusalem. Not long before Jesus was to be crucified, He stopped in for a visit. Mary took some valuable perfume, emptied it over Jesus' feet and wiped them with her hair. Both actions were selfless sacrifices, and the result:

The house was filled with the fragrance. (John 12:3 NLT)

Believers are containers full of a valuable commodity—God's grace, love, and power in the person of the Holy Spirit. He is not to be held selfishly. The next time life gives you a jolt, let the presence of Jesus spill out generously so everyone around you will be aware of His love, grace, and mercy.

What? Me Worry?

Have you ever watched a secular movie and thought, "Wow! There's a powerful Biblical message here, and they don't even know it!" I spotted such a message in the 2015 movie, *Bridge Of Spies*. In the late 1950s a Russian spy, Rudolph Abel, was arrested. James Donovan, an insurance attorney, was assigned by the U.S. government to defend him at his trial.

At Abel's sentencing, Donovan asked him, "Are you worried they will sentence you to death?" Abel answered, "Would it help?" Later, Donovan asked Abel, "Don't you ever worry?" To which Abel replied, "Would it help?"

Finally, Abel was to be exchanged in Berlin for an American prisoner held by Russia. As they stood on the bridge, awaiting the exchange, Donovan asked Abel, "Are you worried how they will treat you after the exchange?" You guessed it. Abel replied again, "Would it help?"

Since I have a tendency to worry from time to time, I really admire that perspective. It's Biblical, of course. Jesus tells us about the futility of worry, *"Can all your worries add a single moment to your life?"* (Matthew 6:27 NLT) The wisdom of Solomon says, *"Worry weighs a person down..."* (Proverbs 12:25 NLT) Let me share some things that have helped me when I'm tempted to worry.

Most worry is about the future, but *all* worry is experienced today. Its only effect is to steal our joy and our peace in the now. Again we can quote Jesus, *"So don't worry about tomorrow, for tomorrow will bring its own worries. Today's trouble is enough for today."* (Matthew 6:34) God says, "Don't worry about the future. I'm already there."

We also worry because we feel unable to handle a situation by ourselves. Moses felt inadequate to carry out God's assignment, and we may feel the same way from time to time. But in Christ, we are more than adequate. *(See Philippians 4:13)* We have His mind and His power.

And we worry when we don't feel in control of our circumstances. We like to be in the driver's seat. The prophet Jeremiah wrote, *"I know, LORD, that our lives are not our own. We are not able to plan our own course."* (Jeremiah 10:23 NLT) In Christ, we can truly leave the driving to Him.

I know, I know. You've heard all that before. But maybe something will click this time and you'll begin to experience freedom from worry. The Bible has more to say and gives us solutions to the worrying problem.

Solution Part 1: Trust, have faith in the Lord. Actually, to worry is the sin of unbelief because we do not trust the One who promised we could trust Him.

Trust in the LORD and do good. Then you will live safely in the land and prosper. Take delight in the LORD, and he will give you your heart's desires. Commit everything you do to the LORD. Trust him, and he will help you. (Psalm 37:3-5 NLT)

Solution Part 2: Pray about everything.

Don't worry about anything; instead, pray about everything. Tell God what you need, and thank him for all he has done. (Philippians 4:6 NLT)

We pray with faith and belief, not doubting God's attention and concern. If we can live by faith and not by what we see, we will experience greater joy and peace.

Solution Part 3: We do our part, counting on God to do His part. When we say, "Don't worry," we don't mean it's okay to sit around and wait for God to do it. We do what we can and then leave the outcome in His hands.

"So don't worry about these things, saying, 'What will we eat? What will we drink? What will we wear?' These things dominate the thoughts of unbelievers, but your heavenly Father already knows all your needs. Seek the Kingdom of God above all else, and live righteously, and he will give you everything you need. (Matthew 6:31-33 NLT)

Our response to, "Aren't you worried?" should always be, "Will it help?" And the answer to that second question is, "Not a bit." So, sing the Bobby McFerrin song, *Don't Worry; Be Happy*. Look it up, listen, and smile.

The WWJD Acting School

You may have seen a WWJD bracelet, bumper sticker, or any of the hundreds of different WWJD trinkets that have been sold. In case you are too young (or too old) to remember, the acronym stands for, "**W**hat **W**ould **J**esus **D**o?"

The purposes for asking this question were either to help in making a decision or to rebuke someone for doing something you don't think Jesus would do. I've heard it both ways.

To ask, "WWJD?" is a step into legalism, not into grace. The church is not an acting school, teaching people how to act like Jesus. When we say, "I think Jesus would do it this way so that's what I'll do," we are consulting our own sense of morality and values and attributing them to Jesus.

The truth is, He conveys *His* sense of morality and values to *us*. To know what Jesus would do was not possible even for those who lived with Him for three years. He was full of surprises and unpredictable actions, always amazing His disciples and everyone around Him.

What the Bible teaches is that we should *be* before we *do*. Then what we do will come from who we are in Christ. Believers are not Jesus clones running around doing everything He did. You are a unique individual with a distinct personality and specific gifts. As you come to understand the working of God's grace in your life, you will simply do things—in your unique way—that reflect the motives and character of Jesus Christ.

Our Christian religious systems often command what we should do (law) at the expense of being who we are in Christ (grace). This was the way of the Pharisees, to whom Jesus said, *"You Pharisees are so careful to clean the outside of the cup and the dish, but inside you are filthy—full of greed and wickedness! Fools! Didn't God make the inside as well as the outside? (Luke 11:39-40)*

We can intensely study scriptures about Jesus until we think we know what He would do in all situations, but we will always fall short. Studying the Bible is important, but life is not in the Scriptures—life is in Him. Jesus said, *"You search the Scriptures because you think they give you eternal life. But the Scriptures point to me! Yet you refuse to come to me to receive this life. (John 5:39-40 NLT)*

To "know" Christ is to have an intimate relationship with Him; so intimate that we automatically express Him in what we do. It is His life lived through us. It is the guidance of the Holy Spirit within. It is resting in Him and allowing Him to lead and empower us in every aspect of our lives according to our individuality and personality.

If you must ask, then the question should be, "Holy Spirit, what would you have me do in this situation according to God's wisdom?"

If you need wisdom, ask our generous God, and he will give it to you. He will not rebuke you for asking. But when you ask him, be sure that your faith is in God alone. (James 1:5-6 NLT; see also John 16:13)

God is not into external behavior modification, but internal life transformation. When we allow Jesus to transform us by the renewing of our minds, we take the gifts we have been given and work them into whatever situation we encounter.

What Jesus did was to be Himself. Now that you are a new creation in Christ, washed clean of all sin, a child of God with everything you need for life and godliness be yourself—your *new* self. This will cause you to naturally do God's will without the need to attend the WWJD Acting School.

Put Jesus Back In The Classroom?

I was cruising through Facebook posts today and came across one that stopped me cold. I guess I've seen it before, but this time I took a closer look. It said, "We need to put Jesus back in the classroom. Type 'amen' if you agree."

This is similar to, "Let's put the Ten Commandments back on the walls in our classrooms," and other similar posts. Bear with me as I look at these two statements that sound good on the surface but crumble to ashes in the light of the New Covenant of grace.

The notion that we can somehow "put Jesus back" in the classroom is very strange. I assume the purpose they have in mind would be to reach those who are unsaved or to get students to improve their behavior. But how would we "put Jesus back" in schools? Perhaps we could give every student a Bible. Maybe having a class on the life of Christ would work. Or we might display a life-size cutout of what Jesus might have looked like. In practice, none of these would accomplish much of anything.

Here's my take: I don't believe that Jesus was ever "taken out" or has ever left the classroom. If He is not there, then there is no student or teacher present who has been born again. It's a fact that as soon as a single born-again believer enters the school building or the classroom, Jesus is there! God's plan is to reach out to people through born-again believers who are filled with the presence of Jesus. Where they are, Jesus is, because He lives in them.

This message was kept secret for centuries and generations past, but now it has been revealed to God's people. For God wanted them to know that the riches and glory of Christ are for you Gentiles, too. And this is the secret: **Christ lives in you**. *(Colossians 1:26-27 NLT; See also Romans 8:10-11)*

The only way to improve the effectiveness of the Gospel in schools—or anywhere, for that matter—is for we who know Jesus to become bolder in our conversation and lifestyle. The reason it may seem like Jesus has left the building is that we Christians act and talk a lot like the rest of the world. Too few of us are obviously different from the unbelievers around us. Instead of Christians transforming the world, the world has transformed a multitude of Christians.

The New Covenant writers often warned believers that in Christ they have been set free from the corruption of the world, that they are new creations, and that they should abandon who they used to be and embrace who they are in Christ. These aren't legalistic commands to obey, but encouragements to be all that they can be as new creations.

Do not love the world or the things in the world. If anyone loves the world, the love of the Father is not in him. For all that is in the world—the lust of the flesh, the lust of the eyes, and the pride of life—is not of the Father but is of the world. (1John 2:15-16 NKJV)

Those who belong to Christ Jesus have nailed the passions and desires of their sinful nature to his cross and crucified them there. Since we are living by the Spirit, let us follow the Spirit's leading in every part of our lives. (Galatians 5:24-25 NLT)

So, putting Jesus back in the classroom is simply a matter of recognizing that when we go into the classroom (or office, or restaurant, or beauty shop), Jesus is there in us. Then we let Him live His life through us, and God's message of reconciliation will be delivered to those who don't know Him.

And all of this [becoming a new person] *is a gift from God, who brought us back to himself through Christ. And God has given us this task of reconciling people to him. (2Corinthians 5:18-19 NLT)*

Now let's look at the idea that things would get better in school classrooms if we would just put the Ten Commandments back on the walls. Well, the New Covenant says the Ten Commandments is, "… *the ministry of death, written and engraved on stones …" (2Corinthians 3:7 NKJV)*

Why in the world would we put the ministry of death in front of young people every day? The Bible says repeatedly that the purpose of the Ten Commandments—the law—is to show people they can never become righteous through their own efforts. *(See 1Timothy 1:9)* There is no hope for righteousness in the law because all it can do is condemn. It was given to point people to the only One who can make them righteous, God Himself.

Here are a few of the relevant scriptures:

For no one can ever be made right with God by doing what the law commands. The law simply shows us how sinful we are. (Romans 3:20 NLT)

God's law was given so that all people could see how sinful they were. But as people sinned more and more, God's wonderful grace became more abundant. (Romans 5:20 NLT)

I do not treat the grace of God as meaningless. For if keeping the law could make us right with God, then there was no need for Christ to die. (Galatians 2:21 NLT)

We can see clearly that the answer to man's sinfulness is not to keep any law or follow a rule book, but to embrace God's grace. God's grace not only provides forgiveness but also provides the desire and power to change our behavior from sinfulness to Godliness.

Sin is no longer your master, for you no longer live under the requirements of the law. Instead, you live under the freedom of God's grace. (Romans 6:14 NLT)

The preceding scripture is so essential to our understanding of Christ's finished work on the cross that I quote it four times in this book. Let it penetrate and dissolve any remnant of religion in your life.

The conclusion is inescapable for any rational mind. Any attempt to change a person's behavior or sanctify society through "putting Jesus back in the classroom" or posting the Ten Commandments on the wall is futile. Change can only take place through believers who recognize their God-given assignment to let Jesus be seen through their lives and their words. The love and grace of God expressed through every believer is God's Plan A to help people escape the corruption of the world and the flesh. There is no Plan B!

Author Biography

Tom Kempf grew up in Minnesota, but he has also lived in Illinois and Massachusetts. He has spent his life as a businessman, a Bible teacher, a magazine editor, and twenty-three years as a church pastor. He was ordained and founded a church in 1987, but he resigned from the church in 2010 in favor of a more casual church expression in homes and with small groups of people.

In addition to Bible teaching and preaching, Tom enjoys flying radio-controlled model aircraft and writing. He currently lives in Florida with his wife, Nancy, and their dog, Mei-Ling.

You may email Tom at *acts2church@comcast.net* if you have questions or comments.

Made in the USA
Columbia, SC
30 May 2017